DAILY MOMENTUM

How to Break Away From Busyness and Shift From Good to Great

Marianne Emma Jeff

Get it Done Diva Press

Book Cover by Lisa McDonell

Editorial Supervision: Lisa Duncan

2nd edition 2024

to all the cinderfellas

In this book, I celebrate many of the incredible women who have inspired me. I also want to take a moment to honor the remarkable men who have supported me along my journey in this precious parcel of time we call life.

To Matt, my dear friend who fills my heart with pride every time he calls me his hero.

To my stepdad, Dave, my adventure companion, for reminding me it's not everyone who writes a book, never mind three.

To my father-in-law, Wayne, who embraced me into the Bitter family, exemplifying the strength of faith and showing me how we can face life's final chapter with dignity and peace.

And to my husband, my steadfast partner in life's dance, who lovingly juggles the daily chores and proudly coined and wears the title of "Cinderfella."

I especially dedicate this book to my dad, Peter, always the heart and soul of the party and the most extraordinary drag queen a girl could ever have. His memory continues to inspire me. I will always be his little darlin'.

> "Little darling, the smiles returning to the faces Little darling, it seems like years since it's been here. Here comes the sun, doo-doo-doo-doo, here comes

the sun. And I say it's all right. Sun, sun, sun, here it comes."

—The Beatles

contents

HABIT THREE | MAKE TOMORROW BETTER THAN TODAY

HABIT FOUR | CREATE SPACE TO BE GREAT

HABIT FIVE | BE CONSISTENT

YOUR DAILY MOMENTUM HABIT

magic

"Staring at the blank page before you. Open up the dirty window. Let the sun illuminate the words that you could not find."

—Natasha Bedingfield

I woke up feeling discombobulated, tired, and overwhelmed. Then I spent ten minutes scribbling messily on a couple of pieces of paper. Afterward, I felt excited, inspired, and energized. While I did sip on my coffee as I scribbled, I didn't deliberately do anything to get myself all revved up. No affirmations or positive talk. I didn't take a special supplement or energy drink. It was just me, my coffee, a few pieces of paper, a handful of questions, and a pen.

To me, that is magic. It is simple, predictable, and ridiculously easy. I use this same process daily, and it still continues to astound me how its alchemy can turn me from one state of showing up in the world into something else. Something better. The "great" version of me!

Some days, I make massive shifts from uninspired to excited in those ten minutes, while others, I move more subtly from bored to optimistic or depressed to slightly sad. I don't deliberately dictate exactly where my journey will take me over those ten minutes. And yet, I know I can always count on being moved forward, upward, and to a more satisfying state, ready to greet the day that awaits me.

I call this process "Daily Momentum," and it has saved my life. I have been practicing and refining it for almost two decades. Daily Momentum has helped me reinvent myself again and again, crystallize brilliant ideas, write best-selling books, win awards for my speaking, and grow my business. Daily Momentum has helped me navigate through days of grief and despair, failure, desperation, and even thoughts of throwing in the towel completely. Like a comforting blanket, Daily Momentum awaits me as I slide out of bed, ready to wrap me in its understanding and acceptance of exactly where I am without demanding me to be anything more or anything less. Daily Momentum clearly shows me, in black and white, evidence that a thought is just a thought—fleeting, ever-changing. How I feel in the morning does not have to be an emotional state I am chained to for the entire day, month, or even the next few minutes. Daily Momentum gives me permission to choose to be great at any moment.

I use the word Momentum a lot in this book. Momentum is that delicious feeling of moving forward to what you truly want. The Daily Momentum process you will learn in this book will allow you to create the momentum not to just be good but to be GREAT at anything you choose to do.

My Daily Momentum practice sets my day in motion. It helps me capture all my exciting ideas so that they don't get buried and forgotten in the busyness of my day. A few pages in my special *Daily Momentum 30 Day Planner*, a handful of questions, and a pen give me the freedom, possibility, creativity, and inspiration to show up ready for greatness day after day. Even on the days when it feels like I am banging my head against the same wall again and again and getting nowhere. Because at some point, I know that Daily Momentum will either show me that it's the wrong wall or help me bust through it to the other side.

My Daily Momentum practice helps me close out my day and makes me feel a sense of accomplishment. I spend a few minutes before going to sleep on Daily Momentum. I sift through the events of the day, celebrate Daily Wins, and remind myself why I am doing the stuff I am doing. Daily Momentum gives me the opportunity to mentally do-over and upgrade what happened throughout the day, so I can make great choices in the future, even if I didn't today.

Daily Momentum allows me to understand not perfection but satisfaction as my measure of success. Daily Momentum keeps my relationship with time, space, and energy healthy on a daily basis. Daily

Momentum gives me a target to aim for. Some days, my target is only a few millimeters away, while other days, my Daily Momentum practice helps me bridge a gap I have fallen short of for years. Daily Momentum allows me to upgrade, evolve, and move forward, even if it may look to an outside observer like all I did was step backward or stumble around in a circle that day. Daily Momentum helps me make sense of things so that I can go to bed with more peace of mind and less itty-bitty-shitty-committee in my head. So that I can be ready to get up the next morning and start the whole thing again...

Daily Momentum gives me strength, courage, and a sense of purpose every day. Through pandemics, grief, success, and obstacles, Daily Momentum has accelerated my personal and professional growth and shortened my periods of learning and failure. It allows me to move forward at a speed that surprises many people around me, earning me the nickname of the "Get it Done Diva."

This book will show you exactly how to use the Daily Momentum process to shift into your Zone of Greatness daily without rushing, pushing, or burning yourself out. I will guide you through all the tools that will make up your Daily Momentum practice and then help you weave those tools effortlessly into your day, so you know exactly how to shift from good to great and make magic daily too!

So, if you are ready, let's get started.

part 1
breaking away

"I want to break free from your lies, you're so self-satisfied, I don't need you. I've got to break free."

—Queen

greatness

You know that feeling when you are in the flow of getting stuff done? You move from task to task effortlessly like a perfectly rehearsed dance. Each individual action is easy. You feel in the zone, laser-focused, like a professional basketball player landing the ball in the hoop from the sideline with a flick of the wrist. Over and over and over again. Each step, each action, and each task perfectly lines up. Stuff just gets done without even trying. You are naturally high. And even before you have completed the project, you feel a deep sense of accomplishment and truly believe you can and will make it to the finish line.

These are moments of pure, unadulterated bliss. This is what it feels like to be in your Zone of Greatness. This is what happens when we break away from busyness and burnout and create the space to shift from good to great.

Unlike busyness, greatness is a state of being, not doing! All you have to do is create space for it and it will show up.

Greatness doesn't happen because we are busy, rushing, pushing, forcing, or coercing ourselves into taking action. Greatness happens when we prioritize a sense of accomplishment, spaciousness, progress, focus, freedom, and fun above just getting results and checking something off our to-do list. When we are in our Zone of Greatness, we can exceed our goals without trying, pushing, or procrastinating. When we operate from our Zone of Greatness, success just happens. We don't have to be busy to be great.

This book is going to show you exactly how to create the space to spend more time in your Zone of Greatness. I use this system myself and with clients to help shift from good to great, every day. You are about to learn how to master what I call your Daily Momentum so that you can spend more time shining your greatness out in the world.

There are many books on the subject of productivity full of hacks to help you squeeze more into the time you have. That is not the purpose of this book. Instead of relying on tricks and hacks that may or may not last, Daily Momentum will show you how to almost effortlessly weave a few simple yet powerful activities into your morning and evening, transforming your personal and professional life and helping you create the space to shift from good to great.

As you begin to spend more time in your Zone of Greatness using Daily Momentum, you will experience more of a sense of accomplishment at the end of every day. You will enjoy more uninterrupted blocks of time to work on projects and make measurable progress. You will quickly see how easy it can be to fully focus on what is in front of you without feeling distracted. And you will learn how to make projects and goals centered around your greatness, your priority, without feeling guilty. As you implement Daily Momentum, you will find the freedom to invest more of your time doing the things you want to do and less of your time on the things you feel like you just have to do.

Greatness is a habit, it is a lifestyle choice, a way of being. Your Daily Momentum practice is the tool that will help you spend more time in your Zone of Greatness so that you can break away from busyness and burnout and shift from good to great anytime you choose.

busyness

A group of friends sit on the beach eating ice cream. Off in the distance, dancing between the waves, they see a woman waving. She looks familiar, and they wave back. They enjoy their ice cream cones and are about to pack up when a lifeguard rushes past them and dives into the pounding waves.

Alas, too late. Just like the last line of a poem by Stevie Smith that has haunted me since junior school English class, she was "not waving but drowning" in a sea of busyness.

If we want to swim, not drown, in the busyness of life, we must create the space to be great. Rushing and pushing our way through life only submerges us further into a cycle of binging, burnout, and not being able to focus enough to become as great as we know we are.

I have worked with men and women for the last two decades who, like you, are high achievers. They are smart, ambitious, and full of brilliant ideas. They show up to work operating from a place of good and they yearn to be great. To them, it feels like all their passion, excitement, and sense of possibility are being held underwater. They feel like they are slowly running out of air, drowning, and I help them breathe into their greatness. Rushing and pushing sucks all the life out of our greatness.

Once you are a high achiever, you always will be at heart. You are never too old or too sick. You never get to retire from being a high achiever. It's how you are wired. Whether you had your own business and now you have a day job or you have achieved all your dreams and goals and are traveling the globe. If you are a high achiever, you always will be; it's in your DNA.

Many high achievers I coach show up embarrassed by their lack of action and feeling like they are falling short of who they really are. They have bestselling books rattling around in their heads but no time to write them. They are curious about technology but often feel like they are behind and can't keep up. They confess to being inconsistent with their actions, often kicking themselves for letting go of opportunities simply because they didn't act on them in time. And they are almost always overwhelmed by projects that they were excited to start but did not finish.

Every day, they sit down with their bottomless physical or mental to-do list and know in their gut that their greatness is drowning in the busyness of their life. I help them understand that greatness is not created by checking off more to-dos. I teach them how to transform how they are showing up every day so that they can create the space to step into their Zone of Greatness.

What if, instead of drowning in overwhelm and burnout, you could leverage the power of your momentum, operate in your Zone of Greatness, and focus like a laser beam on your most important projects?

Feeling good when you know you can be great can feel like life is slipping away like sand between your fingers. On top of that, if you are feeling the pressure to find your purpose and focus on doing things perfectly, it can be paralyzing.

High achievers tend to swing back and forth between busyness and burnout. Busyness is when we are taking so much action that it exhausts us mentally and physically, and it is not sustainable. Burnout is when we are not taking any action, and it usually proceeds a period of action binging or busyness. As the pendulum swings back and forth between busyness and burnout, we may feel an illusion of moving backward and forward, but in reality, we are not going anywhere. For many high-achieving, smart, ambitious men and women, after a while, this constant swinging back and forth is all too much, and they simply drop out of the race.

Not you!

It's not simply a matter of not having enough time. Often, we are so used to rushing and pushing and feeling like we don't have enough time that when we actually find an hour or a hard-earned day off, we experience paralysis. If you quit your day job and started your own business, moved into a new position, or made a big change in your career or life, you may feel overwhelmed because you suddenly have too much time and you don't know what to do. When we are mentally busy, we can feel overwhelmed and confused even when we have lots of time. Many high achievers also suffer from mental busyness. This is when our mind is busy chattering away and figuring things out non-stop. Mental busyness gets in our way of thinking straight and can make us feel like we don't know what to do first or even how to begin.

Once we create some breathing space, our battle is not over. When we have time and space, our natural tendency is to fill it up right away and find something to do. Nature abhors a vacuum, and if we are not careful, we just end up filling our time with whatever is the first thing that comes into our heads. Worse still, we allow someone else to fill it up for us. Daily Momentum will help you develop the habit of being more intentional with your time. And then the breathing space you create as you develop your Daily Momentum practice will not be filled up with everyone else's needs and wants instead of yours. Then you can maximize the time and space when it does begin to open up to create even more space. Think of it as a compounding effect that all starts with owning your day.

Daily Momentum is not aimed at squeezing more out of you using productivity hacks. Hacks only give you an illusion of productivity, success, and space. They are Band-Aids. Daily Momentum instead will give you an onramp to your Zone of Greatness you can use daily.

Daily Momentum will give you the courage to unapologetically focus on the most important things. It will allow you to rise to the level of excellence, service, and mastery that will move you from good to great.

Daily Momentum can help you move beyond paralysis, overwhelm, and burnout. Together, we are going to harness your momentum, unleash your greatness, and achieve the clarity you need to focus like a laser beam and catch your ideas on fire.

Like many men and women I work with, if you are a caretaker—whether for older parents, siblings, children, friends, employees, or even coworkers—then you may be so busy taking care of everyone else that there is little or no time or energy left for your greatness. It's not surprising that you feel like someone else is driving your life and your day.

Today in work and play, we are so overloaded by ideas, suggestions, shoulds, and other people's demands on us that it can feel completely overwhelming and confusing. Most people I coach struggle with boundaries around their time. There is no distinction between when they are focusing on great work or just busy work. Simply spending a few minutes a day on Daily Momentum will give you permission to prioritize your great work. Then, instead of squeezing your stuff in, you can make conscious choices and agreements about what and when you will do for others and what and when you will do for yourself. You can show up fully, with integrity and greatness every day. Don't worry, no one will hate you; actually, you may be shocked by how much respect you earn as you beef up your boundaries and communicate with clarity and confidence.

Daily Momentum will allow you to break away from busyness and burnout so that you can focus on the things that excite and inspire you—great work, great projects, and great goals. And it will allow you to move the important stuff to the top of a shorter to-do list and make it a priority. As you learn and implement your Daily Momentum practice, you will create the momentum you need to have personal and professional breakthroughs. You might finish writing that book, start that new business, get that promotion, or make that move you have been wanting for decades! Daily Momentum is the tool that will help you stop rushing and pushing so that you can cross the finish line and exceed your goals.

What if you could fully implement just one of those brilliant ideas you have knocking around in your head? Your vision of what is possible is inspiring, powerful, and beautiful. I know because I have been coaching smart, ambitious men and women full of brilliant ideas, just like you, for almost two decades. However, an idea alone without action simply makes you a dreamer. Daily Momentum will give you the framework to take action regularly. That way, your dreams don't stagnate or get lost in the shuffle of rushing and pushing. Instead, they shift into action so that you can cross the finish line.

zero gravity

When we start something new, it's normal to feel super excited. High achievers like us love that feeling. Your Daily Momentum practice will help you keep that feeling of excitement so that you don't just sprint at the start and then fizzle out. Daily Momentum will allow you to slow down your action so that you can cover more ground. It will set you up for the long haul, making sure you cross the finish line, not just start the race.

As you begin to implement your Daily Momentum practice, you're going to have moments where it feels like you're barely doing anything. We're going to slow things down, and it may be very different from your usual pace. Think of it like an astronaut in deep space being in zero gravity. Even a small action, like a butterfly fluttering its wings, can lead to a huge surge in productivity.

Sometimes, we overwork our logic, our bodies, or our emotions, and that can lead to burnout. Daily Momentum helps you find the right balance, not leaning too heavily on action alone. Daily Momentum combines the power of vision, passion, and consistent action. It leverages the power of small, consistent actions that add up to big changes, helping you move forward in zero gravity without burning out any part of yourself.

Many of my clients show up hooked on scarcity and urgency, often not starting a project until they feel the pressure of a looming deadline. Sure, we can wing it; but here's the thing: if we are writing a presentation or starting a project a few days before it's due and rushing to hit the finish line, we can't produce great work. Urgency gets you moving, but do you want to be known for producing good work or great work?

If we want to shift from good to great, we need to do more than just the minimum. We need Daily Momentum, not inconsistent action-binging driven by pressure and deadlines. A lot of times, we only pay attention when things are on fire. But the most important stuff isn't always screaming for our attention. If we want to shift out of busyness and burnout, we are going to have to rewire how we operate and maybe even choose not to put out some fires.

The Daily Momentum practice gives us little daily upgrades to rewire our operating system from good to great so that we can function at zero gravity, doing less and achieving more. Instead of grand, sweeping changes, we will be creating habits that shift the small things we do or don't do every day. Daily Momentum shows us how to focus to keep our momentum going, using small, everyday actions to move into zero gravity.

For many of us, Daily Momentum is a game-changer. But watch out—you may get so excited that you might want to make some radical changes. If so, please resist the impulse to get into "doing," "fixing," or even "pushing" yourself to make big changes. Daily Momentum is here to help you get more curious and tap into your Zone of Greatness, to spark new ideas and open you up to new possibilities and options. But be careful you don't start pushing change and, in doing so, create more guilt, overwhelm, and burnout. I encourage you to use any new insights this book creates to step into the place of, "Hmm, isn't that interesting?" rather than creating a whole bunch of new things to do or "shoulds."

Daily Momentum is designed to tap into our natural curiosity so that we create change without even realizing it. It's built around lots of thought-provoking questions. As we begin to ask ourselves those questions, it's important to give ourselves time and space. Pause and simply see what happens naturally before you make any big, radical changes. Trust me, that's the old operating system pushing you, not the great new one moving you into zero gravity. The high achiever in you is used to operating that old, radical way, and you know from experience that it doesn't get you across the finish line—at least not without a high cost.

Instead, Daily Momentum will get you into your Zone of Greatness so that you can let changes happen without all that rushing, pushing, and "trying."

Zero gravity may take some time to get used to. Things may go slower than you would like at first, and you might be eager to jump ahead, especially if you're a personal development junkie or logical thinker. I encourage you to slow down and give yourself the time to acclimatize to zero gravity. It's worth it. The view from greatness is breathtaking.

burnout to breakthrough

I used to get frustrated because I had so many great ideas that were competing for my time and attention. I would take a ton of action every day and still never feel like I was getting anywhere.

Then I pushed myself even harder, completely burning myself out and needing days to recover. I held myself to impossible standards, and I always felt like I was taking one step forward and then 10 steps back!

You see, like you, I am a high achiever. I have always been brimming with dreams, passion, and ambition for as long as I can remember. But no matter how much effort I put in, it always seemed to feel like I was falling short. I'd push myself to the brink only to end up completely worn out. Sound familiar?

Then one day, everything came crashing down. I hit a point where I was so exhausted that I spent nearly six months in bed, with all my doctors scratching their heads trying to figure out what was wrong.

This difficult period was a turning point for me. I realized I was no longer willing to break myself in order to succeed. I knew the projects I wanted to complete would not only give me a deep sense of accomplishment and satisfaction, but they would also impact other people. However, I often felt lost, confused, and stuck, not knowing what to do next.

That's when I decided there had to be a better way. There had to be a way to achieve success without burning out.

So, I read a ton of productivity books, spent over $100K on masterminds, hired coaches, and interviewed over 100 people about productivity. I experimented with the four-hour work week, seven habits of highly effective people, and big frogs. I bought every planner and journal I could get my hands on. And I organized my time and goals in different ways to find a system that worked best.

As I did, I realized...

- Some of the systems felt too regimented and I couldn't stick to them.

- Some systems allowed too much flexibility and no accountability.

- Some systems were way too complicated with lots of unnecessary elements that didn't fit my needs.

So, I started creating my own!

I knew it would have to help me create a blueprint for each day and be a way for me to stay on track and check in with how productive and satisfied I felt at the end of every day. I also wanted a simple process to prioritize that didn't require a Ph.D. and a way to organize all my daily projects and to-dos. I wanted a place to write my most important goals and projects so that they would not get lost and forgotten. And I wanted some really great questions to make me think so that I could learn and grow when I debriefed at the end of each day.

The system I created truly transformed my life. I started achieving the kind of success I had always dreamed of, and it all seemed to fall into place effortlessly. I wrote not one but two best-selling books. My speaking career skyrocketed, bringing me awards and opportunities like speaking at the California Women's Conference and conducting workshops for the Small Business Association.

After I created this system, I wanted to share it with other people like me so that they could benefit from it too. So, I gathered a group of 10 smart, ambitious, entrepreneurial women (whom I admired BIG time) in my living room to see if it would work for them as well.

I led them step by step through the whole system over four hours. I had already used it on myself, but I wasn't sure if it would work for anyone else.

With their feedback, I refined the system so that there was:

- an easy way for them to check in with daily satisfaction and accomplishment

- a method to create uninterrupted blocks of time to work on projects

- a unique approach to staying focused without feeling distracted

- a way to manage overwhelm and procrastination

- freedom and flexibility to quickly schedule each day

- quick and easy daily check-ins focused on the things most important to them

And guess what? They loved it!

Hundreds of people have been using these same tools ever since. And now, 15 years later, I've refined and improved this system to make it even simpler, more powerful, and more accessible. Daily Momentum is a daily practice built around the best, most effective tools I've discovered and shared in my two decades of coaching in business and productivity. And now, it's here to help you break away from busyness and burnout and guide you into your Zone of Greatness.

how to use this book

This book is structured to guide you through different stages of personal and professional growth and shift you from good to great in anything you choose.

Through decades of experience, I have learned that if you want to increase your productivity, success, and satisfaction, then it is more effective to concentrate on refining your daily actions before jumping into big-picture plans and goals. The traditional approach to productivity often urges us to start with big visionary thinking and ambitious lifetime goals. Although I will invite you to think about your dreams and big, brilliant ideas, we will focus primarily on the smaller Daily Momentum in this book. I've learned that starting with day-to-day actions is actually more impactful. When we upgrade our daily productivity, we naturally create more time and space to think more clearly and set more precise and meaningful goals.

Tackling daily routines first doesn't just help us create space for greatness; it also clears our minds and helps us understand what we truly want. If we start with big thinking instead, we might not be in the right mindset to even know what we want. By focusing on our Daily Momentum first, we create space for a clearer, more focused mind, which is essential for setting and achieving larger, life-changing goals and projects. When we do this, the bigger goals may very well simply seem to fall into place on their own.

Greatness is a habit, not a hustle!

This book also includes access to downloadable worksheets and how-to videos. These resources are designed to help you quickly put Daily Momentum into practice and build it into your morning and evening routines. With these tools, you'll be equipped with a hands-on approach to building your momentum every day.
You can access all your Daily Momentum resources at www.dailymomentumhub.com

THE FIVE HABITS OF GREATNESS

You are about to learn all the Five Habits of Greatness.

1. **HABIT ONE: Start Where You Are:** How to let go of

guilt, handle overwhelming feelings, and beat procrastination. Here, we will focus on taking the right action at the right time and making progress step by step in a way that works for you.

2. **HABIT TWO: Know What You Want:** We will tackle distractions head-on. You'll learn strategies to stay focused even when everything seems equally important. This section is about empowering you to stay on track, prioritize effectively, and achieve meaningful outcomes.

3. **HABIT THREE: Make Tomorrow Better Than Today:** Discover tools that will not only help you maintain high-quality work but also find a balance between being productive and taking care of yourself. This section of the book is about achieving remarkable results without losing your joy and peace of mind. You will find tools here to help you become more aware of how you are showing up each day so that you can stop sacrificing your joy now for your joy later.

4. **HABIT FOUR: Create Space to be Great:** In this part, you'll learn to reclaim your freedom, even with a packed schedule. I'll show you how to set clear boundaries to carve out time and space for what really matters to you.

5. **HABIT FIVE: Be Consistent:** This final section is about gaining momentum. You'll learn how to map out a future that aligns with your desires, needs, and goals while keeping

the freedom and flexibility you love.

Throughout this book, I am going to share with you all the tools that make up Daily Momentum. These simple tools, not hacks, can each be used in just a few minutes to zero-in on what you want, take back control of your time, and create space for your greatness. With these tools in your back pocket, you will be able to create more time, space, and freedom in your schedule. Daily Momentum will re-invigorate you and help you gain clarity and that all-important breathing space you need to be great. Even just a small sliver of found time can make all the difference in the world. Pretty soon, that small investment of time will experience compound interest and blossom into days that are full of freedom, space, productivity, and greatness.

Ready to get started? Let's dive in and take a look at the number-one secret to greatness.

part 2

the secret to greatness

"I have run, I have crawled. I have scaled these city walls. These city walls. Only to be with you. But I still haven't found what I'm looking for."

-U2

unlocking greatness

Ninety percent of the time I fall short, do not achieve my goals, or feel like I'm not delivering great work, it boils down to one thing: I simply don't know clearly, specifically, and passionately what I want. I may think I do, but when I stop to really examine why I am falling short, it almost always comes down to the fact that I don't know what I want.

That might sound kind of crazy. How can I be running a business? How can I be operating as a human being on this planet? How can I be living and breathing without knowing what I want? Like many people, a lot of the time, I am running on autopilot. I am taking action without really knowing why. When I am unconsciously responding to people, places, and situations, I am busy, but that doesn't mean I am being productive!

When our focus gets hijacked by other people's needs, feelings, and desires, our own projects can get buried at the bottom of the to-do list. Often, we worry about what people will think if we don't do what they want us to do. We are accused of being selfish if we put our own needs or projects first. The irony is that this belief is a complete contradiction. Think about the premise for a minute. We are being selfish if we don't do what someone else wants us to do. So, it's okay for someone or even everyone else to be selfish, just not us? No one can win with this flawed premise in place.

On top of that, we often feel so busy and overwhelmed that the idea of taking time and energy to stop the runaway train we are on and figure out what we really want feels counterintuitive. And even when we do figure out what we want, it's so easy to get caught up again in busyness and completely forget what we wanted, even if at one point we did know—you know, like when we open the fridge and can't remember what we were looking for. We lose the plot.

For many years, I wasn't just on autopilot; I was literally unconscious of what I wanted. I had no clue. My alcohol addiction meant that I desensitized myself. I turned off my ability to be present in my life, and I spent a lot of time unconscious. My true desires were kidnapped by my addiction. Instead, I focused on when I would have the next drink and what I would drink. Now, don't get me wrong—I was a high-functioning alcoholic. I showed up for my husband and my daughter. I got up and started work at 8 am every day and held down a job. But every night, I downed glass after glass of red wine until I polished off another two-liter bottle, which was never enough.

After I quit drinking, I began to defrost, to feel again. My senses came back. And I had to figure out what I wanted. Just like someone learning how to walk after a car accident, I was a blank slate. I noticed my desires as they popped up and got curious about what I wanted—not just food and drink. What do I want to do? Where do I want to be? What do I want to listen to?

As the noise of my addiction began to slowly quiet down, I saw all the choices life had to offer me, like a delicious buffet waiting patiently for me. My addiction had sucked up all the energy in my life for decades. Everything revolved around red wine and the feeling of being buzzed. Now, I had so many possibilities at my fingertips. I felt a new sense of freedom. I could do things at nighttime when before, it was easier to stay home so that I didn't have to worry about drinking and driving. I realized I had created a prison for myself. Suddenly, I was asking myself one question again and again: what do I want? And I started to realize: I didn't have a clue.

I began tuning into the question more and more. What do I want for breakfast? What do I want to watch on TV? What do I want to wear? I was infatuated by the question, "What do I want?"

What felt satisfying last week is not necessarily going to be the same as what feels satisfying today. We are beautiful, evolving, growing human beings. Figuring out what we want is how we grow and how we become great.

Could you get better at answering the question, "What do I want?" As well as noticing what turns you on and lights you up, you might also notice the contrast of things that you don't want—the things that turn you off, not on, the things that don't feel good. This information is gold! And yes, that is all it is—information. When you experience something you don't want, instead of getting caught up in the emotion of what went wrong—how you got the wrong delivery food, clothes that don't fit, or heavy traffic on your commute—choose to see it as information. Data. As you collect the data of what you want and don't want, you fine-tune your palate.

> Could you get better at answering the question,
> "What do I want?"

As you get clearer on what you want, BAM—you'll notice things just start showing up. Don't take my word for it—experiment with it in your own life. Food is a great place to begin. The next time someone asks you what you want for dinner, notice if you are clear or confused. When everybody's sitting there on the couch scratching their heads, wondering what to eat, observe how quickly food shows up when just one person gets clarity and asks for what they want. And pay attention to how satisfied you are with the food that shows up in front of you. When you know what you want and you get it, food tastes way better!

The secret to greatness is unlocked when you know what you want. It's time to fall in love with yourself, to be in a state of fascination with yourself. Date yourself and become curious about everything. When we first start dating someone else, we want to get to know them. We want to know their favorite color, what they like to eat, and what music they like to listen to. We want to know everything about them. Invest in yourself like you were dating yourself. And just like in a great relationship, the dating phase should never end. Because the question "What do I want?" is never fully answered.

Not knowing what you want isn't unusual; it's actually how most people spend a lot of their time. Look around if you don't believe me. Notice how the words and actions of people often don't line up. If you are foggy and unclear about what you want to eat, where to go at the weekend, or what time to go to bed, then can you imagine how deep the roots of confusion might be when it comes to some of the bigger, more important choices you have in your life and career? In fact, the question, "What do I want?" is at the core of every single choice you have and will ever make in your life.

As you lean more into what you want, you will also begin to see how ridiculously sexy clarity is. When we are crystal clear on what we want—whether it's what restaurant we want to go to or who we want to spend the rest of our lives with—things seem to quickly and effortlessly fall into place. Look around you; notice where there is clarity and certainty and how that draws you in and moves you almost effortlessly forward into action. That's momentum! That's you in your Zone of Greatness.

Think of it like a muscle that you may have not used in a while. Don't worry—it's simple and powerful to reactivate it. All you have to do is ask, "What do I want?" Ask it a lot, ask it all the time, ask it about everything, and whatever you do, don't stop!

Are you ready to approach life with fresh eyes? You have so much greatness to give to the world. To unlock it, just get used to asking, checking in, and truly knowing what you want. Listen for what you want and notice your emotional reaction to it; that's your built-in guidance system. You can use it any time you want to lead you into your Zone of Greatness.

You don't need to begin by looking for the meaning of life; begin with whatever is in front of you. A sense of purpose isn't necessarily about knowing why you are on the planet. It doesn't have to be that profound. Often, your purpose right now may simply be to understand why you are in the room and what you can contribute to the people around you in the next five minutes.

How do you do that? You might be having a conversation with someone, working with a client, watching a TV show, or eating dinner. Keep asking, "What do I want?" The clearer you get, the more you will show up in greatness—not only for yourself and in your work but with your friends and family too.

I used to love the crime TV show CSI. I would watch every single one of the CSI's—Miami, Vegas, all of them. One night, I sat down on the couch with my husband. We got halfway through an episode, and I turned to him. I said, "I think I'm done with this now." I just felt it in my body. I just knew at that moment. I didn't want to watch any more people being murdered. That was it. I completely shifted at that moment. It wasn't just CSI. From that moment on, I had no desire to watch violent movies or TV shows. When something came on, I either changed the channel or left the room. You can do that with anything in your life. You can change your mind about what you want; you can change the channel, and you can leave the room.

After working with hundreds of high achievers, I began to realize it wasn't just me. I have found that the number one reason my clients are not able to achieve their goals is because they do not know what they want but they think that they do. So, let's explore what I mean by that in the next chapter

do you really know what you want?

"I have goals, Marianne, what are you talking about?" This is what many of my clients say when I start asking them what they want.

Yep, I know it may feel crazy, but stay with me here. Trust me, we can be smart, ambitious, high achievers, and think we have goals, but what's really holding us back is not knowing what we want. Even when we set goals, we often don't update them. We raise the bar, change the rules on ourselves, and move the finish line again and again.

Have you ever pushed yourself to focus on too many things at once and just ended up creating more stress, confusion, and anxiety for yourself? Even when we have "set a clear goal," we often end up with so many that we don't really know which goal is most important. Confusion opens the door for doubt, overwhelm, burnout, and procrastination to invade, and this leads to rushing, pushing busyness, and burning out.

We may think we know what we want, but the litmus test is, if we don't feel like we are moving forward, then we don't know what we want. The problem is not that we are lazy and need to push ourselves harder; we just don't really know what we truly want.

Knowing what you want is not as cut-and-dry as it may seem. The tricky thing about defining and knowing what you want is that there are so many layers to it, like an onion. We may feel confident that we know what we want. Maybe it's to write a best-selling book, lose 20 pounds, or launch a new business. But the next layer is why. Why do we want it? Do we buy into and believe our why behind the what?

When we are invested in our goals, projects, and dreams, we believe in them. This is not a fantasized belief that only shows up when we are all pumped up; this is a belief that lasts, that sticks around even when our enthusiasm has run out. It's a deep knowing that makes action a no-brainer instead of having to repeatedly talk ourselves into it.

Think of the exploration of "What do I want?" like the game Marco Polo. Marco Polo is a game kids play in a swimming pool. One person closes their eyes; they are the seeker. The objective of the game is for them to tag the other players without opening their eyes. The seeker yells "Marco" again and again and the other players must reply "Polo" each time. Using the sound of their voices, the seeker must find and tag them. When we ask ourselves again and again,

"What do I want?", it is like yelling "Marco" to find yourself. The game would be boring if the players stayed in the same place, and so, just like them, you are constantly on the move. It keeps things more interesting—trust me. I challenge you to demand to know what you want at every moment. Every moment! To settle for anything less is just that—to settle. Let that sink in.

The Daily Momentum process is going to help you develop the habit of asking yourself what you want every day to ensure you don't get lost, distracted, or slowed down by the confusion of not knowing what you want at any time.

Don't worry, you will get better and better at answering the question, "What do you want?" as you start using Daily Momentum, so be patient with yourself. I'll keep asking, "What do you want?" throughout this book, so you won't forget to keep asking yourself. The answers to this simple yet deep question may not be obvious right away. Often, our heads are so full of requests and demands of other people that our own goals, ideas, and desires are buried deep down, but they are there, I promise you, if you keep digging with the question "What do I want?"

I do want to be clear: Daily Momentum is not simply about figuring out what you want right now and forcing yourself to achieve it. When we try to push ourselves into action, it may work well at the beginning, but after a few months, weeks, or even days, what we wanted when we began may not be what we want now. That's when we may find ourselves procrastinating or starting to feel bored or uninspired. Does this sound familiar to you? This is a sign that we have lost our hunger or desire for what we want. We are always in a constant state of growth. Weekly, daily, and even from minute to minute depending on our mood, circumstances, or environment, we want different things. So, the answer to the question, "What do you want?" is fluid. It may change again and again.

And guess what? That means that all those times you got inspired and created a big grand plan and then later got frustrated at yourself for not following THE plan, it wasn't your fault. It's just that what your big grand plan didn't account for is that you are an amazing, evolving, high-achieving being, ever-changing and growing. As I show you how to set up your Daily Momentum practice, you will develop a lifelong habit of asking and answering some very powerful questions that will increase your clarity and focus. The most important one is to always be asking and answering, "What do I want?"

It's critical to continue to ask yourself what you want in every moment to unlock your greatness. You can't just ask once and be done. "What do you want?" is an ongoing love affair with yourself and how great you really are.

part 3

taming chaos

"I wanna be naked running through the streets. I wanna invite this so-called chaos that you'd think I dare not be. I wanna be weightless flying through the air. I wanna drop all these limitations and return to what I was born to be."

—Alanis Morissette

the weight of greatness

I first met Giselle at a Women's Success Circle I was facilitating in 2006. When she arrived, the group was already deep in conversation about business growth strategies. Giselle entered politely and sat quietly at the back of the room as I introduced the group to many of the ideas I am sharing in this book with you today.

I could see Giselle out of the corner of my eye, sitting quietly, watching and taking everything in. Then suddenly, she couldn't help herself. She put up her hand and said, "How long have you been meeting?" Everyone stopped their discussions, and all eyes were on me.

Giselle was shocked when I replied, "This is our second meeting." The group had already built strong relationships; they had connected. When we connect with other people, we unlock our capacity to be great. And greatness shines like a lighthouse, attracting more greatness to it.

Eighteen months later, I was packing up after our Monthly Success Circle. Giselle had continued to attend regularly every month. I was happy to have her be part of our community, and she made a great contribution to the group. Giselle pulled me to one side and asked if she could chat.

I invited her to sit down with me at a nearby table, and she shared her biggest business challenge with me. "Marianne," she said, "every single week, I am asked to present and share how my company can help people. I know that this would not only grow my business, but this would allow me to help so many more people. But the idea of speaking feels like this massive weight on my shoulders. It makes me feel like I'm pinned to the floor. Can you please help me lift that weight?"

Giselle's not alone. Are you missing opportunities because of fear? Fear is very sneaky. It is not always obvious; fear may not always have you biting your fingernails, cringing in the corner, or hiding behind the couch. Fear can show up as procrastination and being too busy, putting other people's needs above your own, or even addictions to food, caffeine, or binging-watching Netflix.

> "We fear beginnings; we fear endings. We fear change;
> we fear staying stuck. We fear success; we fear failure.
> We fear living; we fear dying."

—Susan Jeffers, Feel the Fear and Do It Anyway

What is fear costing you? Giselle could clearly see that she was losing thousands of dollars in missed opportunities because she was afraid of speaking. It was costing her a lot of energy as she was carrying the weight of worry and regret around about not impacting as many people as she would have liked.

After Giselle shared with me how she was feeling that day, we sat down and came up with a plan to lift the weight that was pinning her down. But before we did, I asked her if she was willing to do three things. I asked her to be vulnerable and open with me. I asked her to invest time to brainstorm, write, and rehearse with me. And finally, I asked her to set and commit to a deadline for when she would speak in front of her first group. I told her that if she did this, it would allow us, over the next six months, to put together a 45-minute presentation that she could use to share her knowledge and experience with people. It would allow us to start to lift the weight of her fear and to make a bigger impact. She said yes.

First, I set up a webinar for her, and I was virtually by her side running all the tech. She was still nervous, but she did great. The next year, she gave that very same presentation sixty times. She graduated from doing it as a webinar to doing it in person as a lunch and learn. Sixty times in one year!

Then the next year, she was invited to speak as an expert in her industry at the state capitol, and she gladly accepted. Remember before, she had been turning down these opportunities because of the weight on her shoulders. Now, the weight had been lifted; she felt confident speaking, and she was having fun doing it. She had invested the time, felt the fear, and done it anyway.

Since that day Giselle first sat down with me and shared her fear 15 years ago, she has continued to step more into her greatness and face her fears again and again. She has grown her business from one office and one employee to dozens of employees and dozens of locations. She has built multiple million-dollar-plus businesses. She has spoken hundreds of times in dozens of countries, including the state capitol and the United Nations.

Every single step of the way, she knew what she wanted. She was working toward a goal. She visualized a successful outcome. She moved from one level of greatness to another, always knowing what she wanted.

Just a few weeks ago, Giselle texted me. She was on Necker Island with Richard Branson. He had invited her to speak, and she quite happily said yes.

fear does not go under the radar

Neuroscientists at New York University and Harvard University in 2009 concluded studies that show people make up to eleven assumptions about someone within seven seconds of meeting them for the first time. This idea gained momentum and became known as the 7/11 Rule. Not to be confused with the convenience store.

What are those assumptions?

We decide their...

1. Education level

2. Economic level

3. Perceived credibility, believability, competence, and honesty

4. Trustworthiness

5. Level of sophistication

6. Sex role identification (their gender identity)

7. Level of success

8. Political background

9. Religious background

10. Ethnic background

11. Social/professional/sexual desirability

According to the study, after those first seven seconds, we then spend the rest of the time looking for evidence to prove whether our original impression is true or not.

Bear with me here as I give you a little more background information from another study so that we can connect some very powerful dots between fear and greatness.

In 1971, in his book, *Silent Messages,* Professor Albert Mehrabian at the University of California in Los Angeles came up with the 7–38–55 Rule. This rule illustrates how people naturally receive meaning and emotion—in essence, how we communicate.

What Mehrabian found was that communication is:

- 7% spoken word (verbal)

- 38% tone of voice (emotion)

- 55% non-verbal communication (body language)

Now, let's look at what all that means when we are dealing with a common fear like public speaking. According to an article in *Forbes*, glossophobia, or the fear of public speaking, affects approximately 25% of the population, including Giselle. Individuals with glossophobia experience mild to debilitating anxiety when speaking in front of small or large groups.

But what does that fear look like? *Healthline Online* states the common symptoms of glossophobia as rapid heartbeat, trembling, sweating, nausea or vomiting, shortness of breath or hyperventilating, dizziness, muscle tension, and a general urge to just get away.

When we feel any of these symptoms, it limits our ability to connect with other people and it shifts us away from our greatness as we withdraw and shut down. Fear in these cases often presents outwardly as widening our eyes, raising our eyebrows, and flaring our nostrils.

Because as we just learned, we make assumptions about people in around seven seconds, and because of Mehrabian's study, we know that 55% of how we communicate with someone is non-verbal—body language—we can conclude that when we are in a state of fear, which looks like widening our eyes, raising our eyebrows, and flaring our nostrils, we can come across as angry, indifferent, bored, disgusted, guilty, or arrogant. These emotions and the body language associated with them typically repel people.

Fear does not go unnoticed under the radar. Instead, it undermines your greatness like cancer.

facing fear

Now that we understand that our fear is not something we can easily hide, let's lean into fear a little bit more so that we can stop it from stealing our greatness.

EXERCISE | FACING FEAR

Grab your pen and a piece of blank paper or a journal and have it close by as I guide you through a few questions.

Write down a few words for each question below. This is for your eyes only. Write freely; you don't need to edit yourself. You don't even need to write complete sentences, just words, thoughts, and ideas that arise as I guide you through a few questions to explore your fears so that we can face them full-on.

1. **What are some of your biggest challenges, obstacles, or problems in your personal or professional life?** What do you struggle with?

2. **How is fear holding you back?** What are you not doing because of fear?

3. **What is your worst nightmare?** What keeps you up at night?

4. **What does this fear feel like?** What are three words that best describe your fears?

5. **What is your fear costing you in time, energy, and money?** Write down a dollar amount.

Take a breath; this is not easy, I get that.

> "...the secret in handling fear is to move yourself from a position of pain to a position of power."
> —Susan Jeffers, Feel the Fear and Do It Anyway

Remember, communication is...

- 7% spoken word (verbal)3

- 8% tone of voice (emotion)

- 55% non-verbal communication (body language)

Fear is one of the main factors that will make or break your ability to communicate, achieve personal or professional success, and build relationships. Can you afford to spend long periods of time in fear?

By being open to the questions in the Facing Fear exercise and leaning into our fears, we began to move toward greatness and away from fear.

the p-word

Remember at the beginning of this section of the book I mentioned that fear is very sneaky. I told you that fear is not always obvious. I shared with you that fear may not always have you biting your fingernails, cringing in the corner, or hiding behind the couch. And I said something else you may have missed:

Fear can show up as procrastination, being too busy, putting other people's needs above your own, and even as a distraction or addiction to food, caffeine, or binging Netflix.

You see, there are more than fifty shades of fear. So, chances are, there is some fear holding you back from your greatness in at least one area of your life. That's why I wanted to address fear face-on before we dive into the Five Habits of Greatness and design your Daily Momentum practice.

The most common way people avoid their greatness is through what is commonly referred to as procrastination. I like to make fun of it and call it "The P-word."

Is there really such a thing as procrastination?

Think of procrastination as just another way of saying "the stuff I didn't do." This play on words softens the emotional charge of feeling like we are "procrastinating." That way, it is less likely to continue triggering our fear. It simplifies things. We are either doing something or we are not doing it rather than the idea of procrastinating being a big, awful disease we have.

Personally, I don't believe that there is such a thing as procrastination. I have a big problem with words like this. These types of labels make us feel like we are stuck in the mud and digging a deeper hole instead of giving us a way of finding our way out. For many people, declaring "I'm a procrastinator" is simply being lazy with their language, not really laziness. We will talk more about labels in the next chapter on the language of greatness.

So, anytime I refer to the mythological beast of procrastination in this book, I'm simply referring to putting things off or not doing things as quickly as you would like to.

We know procrastination is in the neighborhood when we find ourselves getting easily distracted or pulled away from our activities or projects. And if we are not careful, we can generate quite a long list of things that we are not doing.

There are a lot of books that address the idea of procrastination. Bryan Tracy refers to the things we put off as "frogs." In his book, *Eat That Frog,* he invites the reader to "eat the big frog first" and has several strategies to help with procrastination. We can sometimes coerce ourselves into action; however, I recommend not pushing ourselves into action and instead using the tools in this book to understand when we are in our Zone of Greatness and can easily get stuff done, when we are not, and why.

As we go over the Five Habits of Greatness in the following parts of the book, we will cover over a dozen tools to help us troubleshoot and begin to tackle the P-word head-on and eliminate all those distractions, things you are putting off, or frogs.

the language of greatness

About two weeks after I quit drinking, I decided to go to an AA meeting. I was doing great on my own, but I was worried that I was maybe just in the honeymoon phase. What I was doing felt too easy and fun and I began to worry that it might not last.

I had trouble parking outside the meeting and arrived a few minutes after it started. I slipped quietly in the door and found a spot to sit in the large circle of almost 50 people. The exact second I sat down, the person to my left finished saying, "Hi, my name is...And I'm an alcoholic."

I had been attempting to quit drinking for over 20 years and I'd been to many different AA meetings in the past, so I knew the drill. One time, I went to meetings several times a week for a whole year before I fell off the wagon—again. I know from some of the amazing people

I have met over the years in AA that it is a supportive, life-changing organization. And I am sure as I popped in and out of meetings over the years, AA was instrumental in me finally quitting drinking.

But as I sat down in that circle that day, it felt different. It was my turn to say, "Hi, my name is Marianne, and I am an alcoholic," and all 50 sets of eyes in the room were on me. I opened my mouth, but suddenly, I couldn't say those words. I realized in that moment what had empowered me to quit this time—I knew what was different. I knew what had made it so fun and easy not to drink. It was not allowing myself to hide behind the label of "alcoholic." Not because I was in denial; it was the opposite. This time, I was fully owning the delicious feeling of being conscious. I was focused on what I wanted instead of what I didn't want.

To open my mouth and say those words out loud, at that moment, in that meeting, felt like it would jeopardize the joy and ease I was feeling about my future. Perhaps even my sobriety.

So, I surrendered. I opened my mouth, and without any planning or thinking, out tumbled the perfect words. "Hi, my name is Marianne, and I am choosing to live consciously." I focused on what I wanted, not what I didn't want.

Everything in the room stopped. The person next to me just sat, mouth wide open. People coughed nervously, and then finally the person to my right stuttered out, "Hi, my name is…" and the flow of words continued around the circle. A person directly across from me couldn't resist whispering loudly across the circle to me, "You know this is an AA meeting, right?" "Yes," I replied, smiling with a sense of clarity and peace I hadn't felt ever before in my life.

Think carefully about the words you use and the labels you give yourself. Whether it's busy, procrastinator, messy, unorganized, or always late, these are all labels that may very well hold you back. Now, don't get me wrong, I'm not asking you to lie or ignore the truth. Instead, I am asking you to look deeper. Awareness is a powerful magnifying glass that is almost always the catalyst for change.

Many people may still give me the label of being an alcoholic, but I have not had a drink or gotten high in fourteen years. Instead, I have spent that time delighting in what I want, being conscious, and feeling everything. The ups, the downs, and all the in-betweens.

Labels are almost always just another way of making excuses for our limitations. "I'm a procrastinator," "I am not a good speaker," or "I'm messy," are the excuses we tell ourselves. They take up space and are just smoke screens. Greatness is to clearly see who we are and what we want and to create the space for it to show up. It is to live in an excuse-free zone.

Instead of settling for labels, premises, and sweeping statements that disempower you, what if you challenged yourself to understand how you really feel and come up with a different way of saying things? Instead of, "I can't do this," "I don't have any more original ideas," "I don't have enough time," or "I don't feel like it," you can make a little shift that takes all the guilt, shame, and blame away from these loaded statements. "I can't" might shift into the truth of "I don't want to." "I'm messy" might really be, "I'm creative," and "I'm busy" may just be a way of saying, "I have exciting projects I want to work on instead."

There may be a time or place where it feels right to say our new words out loud to other people. Tread carefully—other people might not be ready for your full greatness yet. And, honestly, the most important person you talk to is yourself.

Notice how you talk about yourself. Does it reflect the truth of your greatness? As you step into the language of greatness, you are facing your fears and shining the light on your greatness with confidence, clarity, and creativity, which are all key traits of great leaders.

there is no try

Words hold energy, powerful energy, and science is now acknowledging and studying what that energy looks like and the power it holds. Masaru Emoto did a study on water crystals by placing different words on the front of jars containing exactly the same water from the exact same source. The results were fascinating. Depending on the word that was placed on each jar, the crystals formed completely differently. Considering our bodies are made primarily of water, this poses the question, "What effect are the words I use and surround myself with having on my body?"

As we step into our Zone of Greatness, it's a great time to upgrade our overall vocabulary and look at all the words that are coming out of our mouths as well as the words knocking around in our heads. In the next part of the book, Start Where You Are, we will be diving deeper into expanding our emotional vocabulary, but first, I want to introduce some words to steer clear of—if we want to shift from good to great.

An abundant mindset is built around the meticulous use of words. In the book, *Rich Dad Poor Dad*, Robert T. Kiyosaki teaches the importance of language. His rich dad never used the word "can't," instead replacing it with phrases such as, "I just haven't figured out how yet." Robert T. Kiyosaki tells us that when we say "can't," we shut a door on possibility and change happening and limit the chance of any options showing up. By eliminating the word "can't" from our vocabulary, we leave the door open to all kinds of different choices we might not have even imagined.

Mark Manson's book, *The Subtle Art of Not Giving a Fuck*, brought to my attention how disempowering the word "try" is. The title may feel offensive but don't judge a book by its cover. After reading Manson's book, every time I caught myself using the word "try," I realized I didn't really need it. All "try" did in any sentence was hold me back. "Try" gave me an excuse; it got in the way of me using a much better word instead. So, last year, I challenged myself to upgrade my language and eliminate the word "try." Sometimes it wasn't easy. I was forced to make choices instead of sitting on the "try" fence. But at the end of my experiment, I had created more greatness in my personal and professional life.

Have you ever played a game like Wordle or Scrabble, pondering over each letter to form the perfect word? Wordle is a popular online word game where players have six attempts to guess a five-letter word. We can use a gamified approach to the way we use language in our daily lives too. Think of the challenge of creatively replacing limiting phrases like "I can't," "I should," or "I'll try" with more empowering alternatives, like a game.

We can invest time in the words we choose to articulate our thoughts and intentions in life, turning every conversation into an opportunity to upgrade our language from good to great. The game Wordle encourages us to think outside the box and expand our vocabulary. We can play a game with ourselves to upgrade our language and explore new ways of expressing ourselves, developing more positive and empowering communication.

Think about turning the "can'ts" into possibilities, the "shoulds" into commitments, and the "tries" into actions. By doing so, we not only improve our verbal expression but also reinforce a mindset of positivity and capability in all aspects of life.

If you want to get into your Zone of Greatness, then upgrading your choice of words is a powerful place to begin. You don't have to take on "try" or "can't"; it's up to you. You might find your own no-go words! Simply noticing the words you use will create shifts on its own.

the never-ending to-do list

I get it—if you had just a little more time, a few hours a week, or an extra day, you could be living a very different life. I personally know how frustrating it can be to feel like you only have the time to give 50% of your full potential. You are a high achiever, even if you don't admit it to yourself. Your 50% looks like a lot of other people's 150%. But that doesn't matter because when we know that we are capable of showing up with greatness, delivering anything less feels like we are falling short.

I know we all want to make every minute matter; however, the hustle and bustle of today's hectic world can easily get us off track if we are not careful. Please remember that when I talk about giving 100% versus, say, 50%, I am not talking about rushing and pushing and giving more time to everything. The last thing I want for you is to end up binging and burning yourself out. We all know rushing and pushing is not sustainable. You have already been down that path and bought the T-shirt. Instead, together, we are going to find a new way for you to maximize every minute, drill down to the most powerful actions, and stop trying to be great at EVERYTHING! I will show you how to use zero gravity to live at a higher level of freedom, excellence, and joy that is so satisfying you will become addicted to it. I want to show you how to be in your Zone of Greatness every day!

I spent several decades in the Vicious Spin Cycle (more about that later) of almost making it and feeling like if I could just give a little more of myself, I would succeed. But it was never enough.

I chipped away at my emotional bank account by adding more and more items to my to-do list. I became a multi-tasking ninja. Yet, at the end of every day, I was devastated to find that no matter how hard I worked, I always fell short of my expectations.

Every day, when it was five o'clock somewhere, I would escape my overwhelm by drinking two liters of red wine until I blacked out. Then I would get up the next day a perfectly functional alcoholic and do it all again.

Not everyone who is busy, overwhelmed, and burned out turns to alcohol. Daily Momentum isn't designed to help you get sober, although it did help me. Daily Momentum will help us recognize and understand our addiction to busyness. No matter how much money we make, how many followers we have, or how many best-selling books we have written, there's always room for an upgrade!

When my daughter was born, I was forced to slow down a little. Sofie, my independent daughter, insisted on doing things for herself. We heard "all by myself" about everything, from dressing herself to fastening her own seat belt. I had to step back and give her the time and space to succeed. At first, I felt myself going crazy waiting for her little fingers to perform the task at hand. She would almost close the clasp of the seat belt again and again and again. And I longed to just do it for her and get on the road to the next appointment.

But I waited. And took deep breaths to stop thinking about my long to-do list and tight schedule for the day. I allowed her to take the time to enjoy these moments of independence. I am so glad I wasn't so unconscious that I stole them from her. It shaped what an amazing human being she is today, and it gave me just enough breathing space to eventually begin to see a different way.

Women often approach me for coaching from a place of blame and scarcity. They explain to me that, "It's the economy's fault," or, "I don't have enough time because of..." They start sentences with, "If only..." I gently remind them that we all have the same 24 hours each day and that many women in similar situations, me included, have turned things around and broken their addiction to busyness, burnout, and action-binging.

"I don't have a problem with busyness," you may say. If you feel like you are falling short and not moving toward the things you want, then there is an opportunity for an upgrade.

There is a tendency for high achievers to binge on action—to do a lot of stuff and then just burn out and not do anything for a while. It's like a pendulum that swings back and forth.

Greatness is a way of showing up consistently and taking smaller, even micro-actions that allow us to move forward and break out of the Vicious Spin Cycle instead of just swinging us back and forth to the same spot. I know you can pull an all-nighter and push to get things done; it may even give you a rush. But that is not greatness. It is not sustainable; it is unreliable and inconsistent. And it is the reason we are falling short of our greatness.

Every time I hear someone say, "I don't have enough time," that statement feels like nails on a chalkboard. A lack of time is a delusion. Time scarcity implies that time has been stolen from you, but it hasn't. There is no such thing as someone having more time or less time. Time simply is. It is 24/7 for everyone. It is the choices we make about how we spend our time that create space, freedom, and joy instead of scarcity, lack, and fear.

So often I hear, "I need time. I'll do this once I've got all this other stuff figured out." I'll share some of the tools, like I am doing in this book, and the person I'm talking with will say, "Great, I'll do that once I get projects x, y, and z done." They have it all backward. Until they choose to create space, they will never finish their endless to-do list.

To focus on completing to-do after to-do, desperate to find freedom, space, or time is like drowning and deciding to just keep treading water instead of grabbing onto a life vest. Eventually, you are going to run out of energy to tread water; you have to choose something different today. Do not put off change till you are "ready."

Let's be honest: you will never be ready. There is no "getting it all done," and there is no end to your to-do list right now. But there could be! By the end of this book, I want you to bust the myth of "I don't have enough...". I want you to grab the life vest and choose to learn a new way of showing up each day so that your greatness can shine through.

taking score

Every day, we take score—usually at the end of the day. Unconsciously or consciously, there is a moment when we decide whether or not what we did that day was enough or not. But how do we take score?

A lot of times, we're taking score based on the last few things that happened or maybe some pivotal event. But every day, we do a lot of stuff, and much of it flies under our radar. We are playing a game and keeping score, but it's not a winnable game because we don't know the rules.

I have spent a lot of years being busy, overpromising, and doing too much. It's like an addiction. When instead I under-promise, I have more peace of mind and find I'm able to deliver better work than when I overpromise. So, I invent games to play with myself, to break out of busyness and burnout and shift from good to great. This book is full of tools that I developed from the games I have invented to play with myself.

The first tool I want to share with you is the NOT-To-Do List. It's a simple game I designed because I realized that if there is stuff that I want to do, then I have to choose NOT to do other stuff to make room for it. Whether you take the time to choose or it just happens, some stuff on your to-do list will not get done. Having a NOT-To-Do List makes this a conscious choice.

If we only have a to-do list, all the things on the list are like a chorus chanting, "Do me, do me, do me!" We can't see what's important, and then we typically end up feeling guilty at the end of the day when we don't do some of the things on the list. But we've carried the weight of our long to-do list with us the whole day. The day would be much lighter if we put down the weight of some of the items that are NOT going to get done earlier.

Having a NOT-To-Do List allows us to make those sometimes-difficult choices of what to do and NOT do sooner rather than later. We can consciously decide how heavy or light we want our day to be. As you learn how to create your own Daily Momentum using the tools in this book, you will get much better at knowing what to put on each of your lists. I am going to show you some tools later in the book to help you prioritize and make a better to-do list too. But for now, just thinking about having a NOT-To-Do List is going to help you create more breathing space in your day.

EXERCISE | CREATING A NOT-TO-DO LIST

Every morning, I brainstorm everything that I could do that day. And then I create two lists: a to-do list and a NOT-To-Do List. This creates a powerful choice and allows me to fully commit to the items that end up on my to-do list.

My NOT-To-Do List gives me permission to not do everything.

When we create a NOT-To-Do List, we get to create our own rules and design a winnable game. Maybe you decide that, of all the things you could do today, you will put half on your to-do list and half on your NOT-To-Do List. If that feels overwhelming, start by having one thing on your NOT-To-Do List each day. Then, at the end of the day when you are taking score, you can recognize the things you completed on your to-do list and give yourself points for the things you did not do on your NOT-To-Do List as well.

When you add something to your NOT-To-Do List today, you are saying, "I'm not going to do that today." It doesn't mean you're not going to do it ever; it just means you're not going to do it today. Every item you put on your NOT-To-Do List today will create more space for you to be great—not only today but tomorrow too.

learning to swim

When my mother was a little girl, she never learned how to swim. It wasn't really a concern until one summer vacation with a group of 21-year-old adventurous friends when one person decided it would be fun to throw her into the pool.

What happened next was a stark reminder that learning to swim when you're already in over your head can be a terrifying experience. She sank like a rock and emerged from the water, petrified of it.

At that moment, trying to teach her how to swim would have been utterly useless. It wasn't until she turned 30, almost a decade later, that she mustered the courage to confront her fear.

She signed up for swimming lessons at a local pool, and this time, it was different. Instead of throwing her into the deep end, the instructors took a patient and gradual approach. They helped her build confidence step by step. With each small victory, her fear of the water slowly diminished.

While she may not consider herself a seasoned swimmer today, her once overwhelming fear no longer controls her.

Timing matters.

Learning something new should ideally happen when you're ready and willing to take those first strokes, not when you are drowning. When you are in a place of scarcity and fear, you won't be able to think clearly about the best strategy.

Instead, it's better to develop a habit of spending a little time each day on small, specific, micro-actions that can help you build new habits to shift from good to great. Plant seeds, water them, and enjoy the harvest later.

This book isn't designed to throw you into the deep end; instead, it will provide you with the simple tools and clear daily actions to help you gradually build your confidence day by day.

Whether you're a professional looking to advance your career, an entrepreneur, or a stay-at-home mom, this book is designed to meet you where you are—because everyone has their unique journey, just like my mother did with her fear of water, and because everyone has the capacity to be great.

Now that you have learned how to tame the chaos of fear, procrastination, labels, language, and your never-ending to-do list, it's time for us to start getting familiar with the Five Habits of Greatness and all the tools you can use in your Daily Momentum. Let's begin with Greatness Habit One: Start Where You Are.

HABIT ONE

start where you are

"Come as you are, as you were, as I want you to be, as a friend, as a friend, as an old enemy."

—Nirvana

step on the mat

I arrive at the studio and unroll my mat. A few minutes later, the teacher walks into the room. She flips the switch to turn on the fluorescent lights, and we all jump to our feet. Each of us steps onto our mat. It doesn't matter how well we did yesterday or the day before; we all know we must start where we are today.

We move obediently through the challenging postures of balance, stamina, and determination. Bikram yoga is an intense, steamy, sweaty practice. After almost six months of daily practice, I have a love-hate relationship with each pose. It's always the same 26 poses in the same order. I curse inwardly as I struggle to maintain half-moon, the most torturous pose for me right now. Sweat drips off my nose onto my knee as I balance in eagle pose, and I smile as I raise both legs off the ground, making what had felt impossible only a month ago possible in locust pose.

My mind wanders, and I think about my dad, who was an athlete. He played soccer into his sixties with men much, much younger than him. He sweated as he strode across the football pitch, heading the ball into the goal with ease like a beautiful ballet. When I was born, my mum hated that soccer stole so much of his attention. The day I was born, he kissed me and ran off to play soccer. He left my mother alone, confused, and wondering what this strange thing was in her arms.

I, on the other hand, was no athlete. In beach volleyball, the teacher called me "Princess." I forged sick notes to avoid PE, and my training for a 5k involved drinking till 2 am and smoking 40 cigarettes. And yet, here I was, addicted to hot yoga!

As I moved into tree pose, I faced off with myself in the mirror, my eyes landing on my third eye. "I see you," something within me whispered. I realized suddenly that after six months of daily practice, I was getting stronger and more dedicated. I could feel the adrenaline of exercise and was craving it. Is this what it feels like to be an athlete?

I felt a strong wave of emotion sweep over me as I lay down on the ground for the floor series and a deep connection with my dad. I never truly understood his passion for playing football and running from pier to pier on the beach. As I moved with strong focus into the next poses—cobra, bow, and rabbit—my emotions felt like they were beginning to break out of their cage inside me.

My dad had been diagnosed with Huntington's disease a few years ago. It is a cruel combination of Parkinson's disease, ALS, and

Alzheimer's all in one body. I suddenly and clearly understood the intense loss my dad must have felt for not being an athlete anymore. To feel so unsteady and weak after a lifetime of strength and agility must feel like losing yourself.

I felt tears on my cheeks and gathered my focus back on my breath as I tried to twist my back like a pearl necklace, the teacher's voice guiding me. As we did our last sit-up and kneeled on the mat for our final breathing exercise, the breath of fire, I struggled to hold it together.

The teacher methodically clapped the cadence of our breath for us. I fell into the rhythm and fell apart. A deep primal cry came up from my belly. It shook the room and certainly shook me. Suddenly, I was no longer in control. I sobbed like I had never sobbed before and had always wanted to. The deep release felt so good. I surrendered and just let the waves of emotion sweep over me like an orgasm.

I didn't care that this was not one of the poses; I didn't care that I was in the middle of yoga class. At that moment, maybe for the first time in my life, I truly didn't care what anyone thought of me.

As the class ended, I lay on my mat, sobbing. The teacher came and kneeled by my side. "This moment is a gift," she told me. I felt the sacredness of the moment between us. She held me as the last waves of emotion subsided. Knowing just when to leave, she stood up and walked out of the room. I rose, feeling lighter. "You did that for all of us," one lady told me as I left the studio. "Thank you," she said. I smiled. Everything was all right. There was no need for words.

You may not need to break down to move forward into greatness, but you will need to step on the mat so that you can start where you are.

your emotional scale

How do you feel, right now? More than likely, you will answer with a four-letter word: "Good." Thought leader Abraham Hicks created a powerful scale to help us expand our emotional vocabulary beyond "good." It's called the Emotional Scale and is included in the book, *Ask and It Is Given: Learning to Manifest Your Desires*. The Emotional Scale is simply a list of 22 words to help you identify how you are feeling at any given moment. It is a great way to help you start from where you are.

When a woman wants to get pregnant, she is often encouraged to take her temperature frequently throughout the day to learn more about her cycle and when she is ovulating. Then she can align with her cycle to create life!

In the same way, starting where we are and measuring how we feel helps us discern the best time to focus on different projects or tasks. This can give us valuable feedback to help us create more productivity and satisfaction and align with the greatness in our lives.

In this chapter, you will learn how to use the Emotional Thermometer (a tool I created based on Abraham Hicks's Emotional Scale) to take your emotional temperature throughout the day so that you can clearly identify how you are feeling. At the bottom of the Emotional Thermometer sits fear. Further up, we find anger, doubt, and overwhelm. At the top end, we find bliss. And right at 72°, we find the sweet spot—satisfaction, or we might think of it as contentment. Satisfaction is the turning point where we shift from good to great. 72° is the most satisfying level of heat on the thermostat for most people in terms of heat in their home. Think of the Emotional Thermometer in the same way. If you find yourself at 72° (Satisfaction) or above, you are in your Zone of Greatness.Anything below 72° (Boredom, Fear) means you are not in your Zone of Greatness.

As you gain a better understanding of when you are in your Zone of Greatness and when you are not, you will see that this directly correlates with when is the best time to work on important projects. Taking your emotional temperature will also help you to better understand when you are not in the Zone of Greatness so that you can know when it is time to take a break.

Just finding words to describe how we feel in any given moment allows us to start where we are, no matter where we sit on the Emotional Thermometer. If we simply take the time to ask ourselves, How am I feeling right now?, we can wake ourselves up and shift our energy in moments, not months.

Noticing I'm a little frustrated right now doesn't mean we have to instantly push ourselves to feel joy. We don't need to be a Pollyanna and paint everything with unicorns and rainbows. Instead, the Emotional Thermometer is a tool to be honest and truthful about how we are feeling rather than ignoring these opportunities for insight and growth.

When we are using a GPS to give us directions, we first have to plug in where we are. Otherwise, the directions we receive from the GPS won't make any sense. If we deny where we are in the moment, even if we get directions to move forward, they won't work. That's why often what works for someone else won't work for you. We are all starting from different places.

Our inner guidance system or intuition functions just like a GPS system. When we focus on starting where we are, we will find that the right directions, nudges, and ideas show up, and following them becomes much easier.

You can take your emotional temperature every morning and notice how you are feeling as you step into the day. Before you sit down to work on a project, get into the habit of taking your emotional temperature. That way, you will quickly identify if this is the best time to work on the project at hand. Taking your emotional temperature gives you full permission to Start Where You Are, right now! No judgment.

Create a habit of taking your emotional temperature throughout the day. Find ways to attach this new habit to routines you already have throughout the day. Maybe after lunch, when you finish brushing your teeth, or after walking the dog.

I would suggest that you take your emotional temperature at least once a day. Create a habit of checking in with yourself each morning. The Daily Momentum process has this built into it, so don't worry I'll show you exactly how to incorporate it seamlessly into your day later in this book.

And whatever your emotional temperature is when you take it, keep in mind that it doesn't mean you have to stay at the same emotional level all day. Think of emotions as energy in motion. Let's say we are feeling overwhelmed. If we acknowledge that first thing in the morning, we will probably move forward beyond overwhelm and maybe begin to feel a little bit of boredom. That's up next on the Emotional Thermometer. As we become more familiar with the 22 emotions on the Emotional Thermometer, we quickly see that boredom is an upgrade.

Eventually, it won't really matter to you where you are when you take your emotional temperature. You can simply use the Emotional Thermometer to help you acknowledge if you are in the Zone of

Greatness or not. Then you can use some of the other tools I am going to share with you to move yourself into your Zone of Greatness.

The Emotional Thermometer

100° LEVEL 1 | BLISS: Joy, appreciation, freedom, and love. Boundless energy and unconditional love, where freedom and empowerment merge.

95° LEVEL 2 | PASSION: A surge of dynamic energy, driving you toward your passions with fervor.

90° LEVEL 3 | ENTHUSIASM: Eagerness and happiness. A lively state of joy and keen enthusiasm, ready to embrace life's adventures.

85° LEVEL 4 | BELIEF: Positive expectation. A firm conviction in positive outcomes, paving the path for future successes.

80° LEVEL 5 | OPTIMISM: Bright outlook. An optimistic view that illuminates possibilities and opportunities ahead.

75° LEVEL 6 | HOPE: Hopefulness. A gentle anticipation of good, sensing the promise of better things to come.

72° LEVEL 7 | SATISFACTION: Contentment. A serene acceptance and satisfaction with the present moment.

70° LEVEL 8 | BOREDOM: Stagnation. Feeling stuck in place with a dull sense of disinterest in the surroundings.

65° LEVEL 9 | NEGATIVITY: Pessimism and shadowed thoughts. A dim outlook where negativity begins to cloud judgment.

60° LEVEL 10 | FRUSTRATION: An uncomfortable eagerness for change marked by irritation, restlessness, or impatience.

55° LEVEL 11 | OVERWHELM: Swamped. A sense of being engulfed by too much at once, leading to stress and anxiety.

50° LEVEL 12 | DISAPPOINTMENT: Letdown, the sinking feeling of unmet expectations or hopes.

45° LEVEL 13 | DOUBT: Uncertainty that casts shadows over confidence and decisions.

40° LEVEL 14 | WORRY: Persistent anxiety that disrupts peace of mind and clarity.

35° LEVEL 15 | BLAME: A sense of being the victim and harboring resentment.

30° LEVEL 16 | DISCOURAGED: Disheartenment. A loss of spirit and motivation, feeling discouraged by circumstances.

25° LEVEL 17 | ANGER: Fury that demands immediate expression and release.

20° LEVEL 18 | REVENGE: A deep-seated desire for retribution, fueling negative actions and thoughts.

15° LEVEL 19 | HATRED: Intense hostility and wishing harm upon others.

10° LEVEL 20 | JEALOUSY: Envy. Coveting what others have, accompanied by feelings of inadequacy.

5° LEVEL 21 | SELF-DOUBT: Insecurity, guilt, and unworthiness. A chilling fog of uncertainty that clouds our ability to make decisions.

0° LEVEL 22 | FEAR: Grief, depression, despair and desolation. Hitting bottom, marked by a sense of utter powerlessness.

EXERCISE | TAKING YOUR EMOTIONAL TEMPERATURE

Take your emotional temperature right now.

Just noticing which level you're at right now, in this moment, will allow you to better understand your emotions and help you raise your emotional intelligence, which we are going to talk more about in the next chapter.

Right now, you might be at level eleven—overwhelmed—or you might be feeling excited and passionate, which is level two. Maybe you feel hopeful (level six) or you might feel a little frustrated because you have forgotten your password and can't log into your email account, that's level ten. It sounds crazy, I know, but taking the time each day, maybe even several times a day, is going to help you understand when you are in the Zone of Greatness and when you are not.

1 BLISS | 100°
2 PASSION | 95°
3 ENTHUSIASM | 90°
4 BELIEF | 85°
5 OPTIMISM | 80°
6 HOPE | 75°
7 SATISFACTION | 72°
8 BOREDOM | 70°
9 NEGATIVITY | 65°
10 FRUSTRATION | 60°
11 OVERWHELM | 55°
12 DISAPPOINTMENT | 50°
13 DOUBT | 45°
14 WORRY | 40°
15 BLAME | 35°
16 DISCOURAGED | 30°
17 ANGER | 25°
18 REVENGE | 20°
19 HATRED | 15°
20 JEALOUSY | 10°
21 SELF-DOUBT | 5°
22 FEAR | 0°

When you take your emotional temperature, identify which level best describes how you feel at that exact moment, not how you want to feel. The beauty of taking your emotional temperature is that how you feel in one moment is not how you're going to feel in the next.

Change is the only constant in life. If you want to increase your capacity for greatness, then I encourage you to start expanding your emotional vocabulary by taking your emotional temperature regularly. This self-awareness will create reference points throughout your days and weeks. The Emotional Thermometer will help you upgrade the words you use to describe how you are feeling and move beyond okay, good, and "same old, same old" to great.

It's important to note that when we feel a lot of negative emotion or resistance, it is better to focus on something else until we "feel" lighter and have moved further up the Emotional Thermometer.

Sometimes, we don't know we are overwhelmed because we are so used to feeling that way. When we pause to take our emotional temperature, it gives us a way to check in with ourselves and even gives us the language to describe how we are feeling.

After I quit drinking, I was very out of touch with how I was feeling after decades of numbing myself. I didn't know what felt satisfying and I wasn't able to notice very quickly if I felt sad, angry, or overwhelmed. It took time for me to thaw out, and the Emotional Thermometer really helped me in that process.

Let's look at some examples of how we can use the Emotional Thermometer to increase our productivity and satisfaction.

Create a habit of taking your emotional temperature in the morning as you start your day. Then build your day around how you are feeling, as much as you can. For example, if you are feeling discouraged, then maybe that's not the best time to make sales calls, ask for a raise, or have a difficult conversation with a family member. Use some of the tools I am going to share with you in this part of the book to raise your emotional intelligence. You can also move those tasks to later in the day or another day completely if you can.

Notice if a potentially negative craving, need, or impulse shows up. Perhaps you have an urge for a piece of chocolate cake, chips, or maybe binge-watching Netflix. Pause and take your emotional temperature to help you discern if the craving is a need you can choose to satisfy or a reaction to a negative emotional state. Sometimes simply realizing you're bored will allow you to choose greatness instead and close the refrigerator. Then you can call a friend or go for a walk rather than eating the chocolate cake.

Look out for the P-word. The word "procrastination" is thrown around a lot these days, and as I shared with you in the part of the book focused on Taming the Chaos, I don't believe in it. If you are labeling yourself as a "procrastinator," it may be that you are just being lazy with your language, not your actions. If you are not doing what you want to do, then take your emotional temperature. Acknowledging that you are angry, worried, or jealous may give you ideas about how you can shift into your Zone of Greatness without pushing yourself. Don't be surprised if just the act of taking your emotional temperature evaporates your so-called procrastination instantly.

Don't underestimate the power of this simple tool. Taking the time to notice how we feel in each moment can in itself lift and change our mood. Using the Emotional Thermometer, not only do we recognize where we are right now, but we can also see the pathway to the next emotion above. This allows us to understand our emotional state and manage our behavior better, which are both characteristics of having high emotional intelligence—EQ. We are going to learn all about that in the next chapter.

Included in your free resources at www.dailymomentumhub.com, you will find your first productivity-boosting tool: Your Emotional Thermometer.

your emotional EQ

In the world of self-improvement and personal growth, emotional intelligence is one of the most recent breakthroughs. Dr. Travis Bradberry's and Jean Greaves's research published in their book, *Emotional Intelligence 2.0*, offers deep insights and practical guidance to help us understand and upgrade our emotional intelligence—or, as they refer to it, EQ.

Emotional Intelligence

Emotional intelligence is defined by our ability to recognize and understand emotions in ourselves and other people and how well we use this awareness to manage our behavior and relationships. Emotional intelligence affects how we navigate social situations and scenarios. It also influences how we make personal and professional decisions and how well we achieve results.

Emotional intelligence is referred to as EQ, in much the same way as intellect is referred to as IQ. Since our brains are wired to make us emotional creatures, our first reaction to an event is always going to be an emotional one. Yet, when we are looking to improve our productivity, behavior, or habits, we often skip how we feel and jump right to thinking instead and trying to "fix" things.

In the first Habit of Greatness, Start Where You Are, we will unlock the full potential of Emotional Intelligence—not just as a concept but as a skill we incorporate into our daily lives. That way, you can build emotional intelligence into your Daily Momentum, which you will put together in the final section of this book. Starting where you are means to enhance your self-awareness and develop greater self-regulation so that you can use emotional intelligence to spend more of your time in your Zone of Greatness.

There's no getting away from emotional intelligence. It is not something we can ignore; it's built into our operating system. We have no control over our initial emotional reaction to events and experiences in our daily lives. And there's nothing wrong with feeling emotions. When we start where we are, we don't eliminate emotions. Why would we? Eliminating emotions such as fear, overwhelm, or anger would also eliminate joy, happiness, ecstasy, and excitement. Instead, if we focus on starting where we are, we can acknowledge any and all emotions and then make a conscious choice if we want to move beyond them. While you cannot control your initial emotional gut reaction. you absolutely can control the thoughts that follow after. You can control how you think about your emotions.

Remember Professor Albert Mehrabian at the University of California in Los Angeles whom I mentioned earlier? Let me remind you. His research found that communication is actually only 7% verbal, spoken word (what we say), 55% of communication is non-verbal (body language), and 38% of the time, we communicate using our tone of voice (emotion). Communication is what we do all day unless we are living under a rock. We communicate at work, with loved ones, and in social situations. Take a moment to think of all the great leaders you admire. It is likely they are or were great communicators. Communication is how we shine our greatness the most. The higher our EQ, the better we communicate.

In *Emotional Intelligence 2.0*, the authors learned from their research that two-thirds of us have very low EQ. That means two out of three people are primarily controlled by their emotions but are not yet skilled at recognizing them and using thought to move beyond them.

In those same studies, they also discovered that for every point that you increase your emotional intelligence, you add $1,300 to your annual salary. The maximum EQ score is 104, the average EQ score is 75, and 140 is considered to be very good. Simply by finding ways to increase our emotional intelligence, we can increase our paycheck considerably, even if we are the ones writing the check.

Emotional intelligence is also a powerful way to increase our focus with tremendous results. In the process of improving our emotional intelligence, we find ourselves upgrading our time management, decision-making, and communication skills.

EQ scores are also an important success factor. According to co nsciousdiscipline.com, in all types of jobs, EQ is the single biggest predictor of performance in the workplace and the strongest driver of leadership and personal excellence.

Let me remind you again what emotional intelligence is: your ability to recognize and understand emotions in yourself and other people and your ability to use this awareness to manage your behavior and relationships. These are all skills essential for high achievers to be able to function at their best. Our level of emotional intelligence affects how we navigate social situations and scenarios, and it also influences how we make personal and professional decisions and how well we achieve results.

There are four quadrants of emotional intelligence:

1. Self-Awareness

2. Self-Management

3. Social Awareness

4. Relationship Management

In the next chapter, I'm going to show you a ridiculously simple tool that will help you upgrade your emotional intelligence in the quadrant of self-awareness.

Take a breath, and make sure your feet are on the ground so that you can start where you are. That way, you can make sure you are getting the most out of all the insights and tools that I'm about to share with you.

wins

Many people use a gratitude journal or daily appreciation as a way to make themselves feel better. Instead, I like to take the time to acknowledge my WINS. This is also a great way to take inventory of what happened and where you are right now, whether it's for the day, the week, or the year.

When I give myself the space to acknowledge and celebrate my wins, I find it is a powerful way of shifting how I feel—often more so than simply practicing gratitude or appreciation alone, although these are great tools as well.

We can celebrate wins in any and all areas of our personal and professional lives. A win might be in the area of love, self-care, or spirituality. If you meditated for a couple of minutes, learned something new, or played a game, those could all be counted as wins for you. We can celebrate wins in the areas of family, friendship, community, money, or our physical environment. Maybe you tidied up your desk; that's a win.

We can have wins that are financial, a great idea, or developing a new habit or routine. Wins can be experiences we have, opportunities, or even things we didn't do—remember the NOT-To-Do List?

In the Daily Momentum process, you will create a habit of writing down three wins every day. We will get more into that in the section on Daily Momentum.

3. Daily wins

What did do you do today that you can celebrate?

1. ....
2. ....
3. ....

The biggest pitfall with this little tool, however, is that we may very well think too big. A win is not that we got to the top of a mountain; a win is that we took the first step or the next step. So, if we are going to climb Mount Everest, then we get to celebrate the win that we booked our flight. We get to celebrate the win that we packed our backpacks, and we get to celebrate the win that we went to the gym to train for 60 minutes. We can also celebrate the win that we ordered the food that we're going to use for the trip—you know, all that freeze-dried yumminess.

So often we think that we can't celebrate a small step toward a big project or goal as a win. But we don't have big wins nearly as often, so if we only give ourselves permission to celebrate big wins, we don't experience a feeling of accomplishment every day. And we need that to create momentum.

Wins are all of these little micro-steps we take that get us to the big things that make us great. Without the small steps, we would never arrive. When you start to acknowledge the little wins, it may feel ridiculous at first. That's when you know you're probably doing it right.

Any day you are struggling to come up with three wins, then you're thinking too big. We all have at least three wins every day. And that is a very conservative estimate. When you feel stumped by this question, challenge yourself to keep thinking of smaller victories and accomplishments to celebrate until you have three. When we do begin to acknowledge wins, we start to shift how we feel. Wins are like emotional foreplay and raise our EQ. When we realize what we have accomplished and we celebrate it, we naturally start to move up the Emotional Thermometer and into our Zone of Greatness.

We can stop and recognize wins anytime we need a little bit of an emotional boost. Maybe simply writing down three wins will be just what you need to move you from a place of overwhelm into a place of hopefulness.

Celebrate wins anytime:

- What are your wins from this morning?

- What are your wins from your workday?

- What are your wins this evening?

what do you expect?

I have an incredibly positive mindset, but don't get me wrong—I don't just gloss over the negatives in life. I truly feel positive and happy most of the time. This is a huge achievement coming from someone who suffered from depression and attempted suicide twice before the age of 21. I'm not a Pollyanna spewing annoying positive words and underneath it all being unhappy. I only speak truths; I speak what is true for me.

This last year has been a challenging one with both the death of my father after suffering for over a decade with Huntington's disease and the death of my father-in-law after a courageous battle against pancreatic cancer. Daily Momentum allowed me to be honest and present in the emotions I was experiencing and to manage my response to the feelings of depression that arose.

There are also days, many of them over the last decade, when I walk around the house and I feel so good I can't help expressing it out loud. Honestly, it is not important to me whether anyone hears me or not. My husband is used to me walking around saying, "I feel so good right now." It is not every minute of every day, but when I do feel good, I milk the hell out of it.

I wasn't born this way; this is a muscle I have exercised over decades, and Daily Momentum has been a huge help. I have become diligent about catching myself when my language does not match how I feel. I now notice when I am moving into the lower end of the Emotional Thermometer much sooner than I used to, and I use the tools I am sharing with you to move myself back up into my Zone of Greatness. Because of this, I have been able to upgrade my expectations, and now I have higher expectations and standards for myself.

I simply refuse to go back to my old operating system of rushing, pushing, binging, and burning out. Instead, if I am feeling sad, I use the Daily Momentum process to ask questions to create some traction, but I don't push myself to deliberately change how I feel. I ask questions like, "What do I want?" and, "How do I feel?" in earnest because I truly have faith that when I do, it opens up more possibilities for me to choose from in the future.

I used to be really good at expecting the worst. I would worry about what might happen, get angry about how I thought someone was going to respond, or I would feel sad about an upcoming experience before it had even happened. We all carry expectations around with us about EVERYTHING. Most of the time, our expectations remain unspoken, locked in our minds. Yet, they impact how we feel and can leave us feeling unfulfilled, unproductive, or unsatisfied day after day.

Recently, thanks to the teachings of Michael Neill and his podcast *Caffeine for the Soul,* I came to realize that those thoughts and suicidal ideations I used to have in my mind were just my way of handling stress, fear, and overwhelm. Nowadays, instead of drinking into unconsciousness, or overdosing on pills when I feel negative emotions or stress, I choose to use my emotional intelligence and invite myself into my Zone of Greatness.

Our expectations are our imagination in action. But when we are using our imagination to expect the worst, we are working against ourselves and away from our greatness. We can choose instead to use our imagination to expect something different and shift our emotional state anytime we want. We can use questions to daydream about the things we want or worry about the things we don't want. When we start to understand the power of emotional intelligence, we catch ourselves quicker when we are worrying. We can ask questions to shift ourselves into different thoughts which in turn shift how we feel in that moment.

Every time I catch myself worrying or on the lower end of the Emotional Thermometer and turn it into a question, I am inspired to create something different in response. Something better. When we realize we are feeling frustrated, we can decide to get rid of some of the things on our plate instead of rushing and pushing. Maybe when we notice we are feeling overwhelmed, we can review our schedule and move projects out a little further to give ourselves more breathing space. If we are feeling disappointed, we might choose to give ourselves permission to drop the perfectionism on the projects that matter to us less so that we can bring more focus, attention, and greatness to the things that matter to us more.

We imagine change before it happens. We create the future in our minds first. As you begin to tune in more to using your imagination and shift your expectations for your future, you may also notice how your own expectations influence how you interact with other people. For example, have you ever been on your way to meet a friend and imagined they were going to be sad, mad, or excited before they showed up? We might even give them a label like "always late" or "complainer." The more experience you have in understanding your emotions, the more you will begin to open up to different scenarios and possibilities for greatness you couldn't see before. We can instead choose to expect to see greatness in other people, and ourselves, no matter what the past or present circumstances.

We may not think of ourselves as creative, but it doesn't matter; we all have imagination—it's built-in. If we bake a cake when we put the cake in the oven, we can imagine what the cake will look like once it's baked. And as we smell it baking, we can almost taste it before we even take it out of the oven. This is our imagination at play. Think of preparing for a special evening or event in the future. Imagine how it's going to look, picture the table set. Who will be there? Imagine yourself in that moment. You see, we already use our imagination all the time.

We get what we expect, and our imagination is the software we can use to expect more greatness in our future. Start where you are, and take your emotional temperature, and then you can use questions to spark your imagination and create new, exciting possibilities and expectations. In the next chapter, we are going to do just that.

activate your imagination

Everything that you have ever achieved began as an idea in your imagination. And as a high achiever, I know you have achieved a lot, even if you don't recognize it. Your business, your career, your amazing vacations, your home, and the accomplishments you are so proud of each began as a desire. Ideas, given the freedom to grow in our imagination, are the seeds of our future.

The next exercise will help you raise your emotional intelligence, nurture your imagination, and help you get better at knowing what you want.

EXERCISE | ACTIVATING YOUR IMAGINATION

I'm going to guide you through some questions. I want you to write a few words for each question. This is for your eyes only. It might be tempting but don't share the desires and dreams that may emerge with anyone else just yet. You don't need to edit yourself as you are writing or write perfect sentences; just allow words that drop into your mind to be written onto the page in front of you as I ask you the following questions.

1. **What are some of the biggest opportunities available to you right now?** Trust me, they're there. If the word "biggest" in that question stumps you and you can't think of anything, just cross out the word "biggest." What are some of the opportunities that are available to you right now? Places you could go? People you could connect with? Conversations you could have?

2. **Which of these opportunities feels the most fun for you?** And why does it feel fun? It may feel fun to lean into the opportunity of improving your networking skills or maybe how you are managing employees. Maybe writing feels fun, going on a cruise, or volunteering overseas. Perhaps speaking and sharing your story or expertise in a podcast or video feels fun. Write down what feels fun to you. After you have finished, continue to write about why it excites you until you feel complete.

3. **What do you dream about?** What do you see or imagine in the future? What are your wildest dreams?

4. **How would the future that you're imagining contribute to you in time, money, and energy?** Will the

future you are imagining fill you up? How much money would it create if you did write that book, finish that project, speak to that group, or realize your wildest dreams? I want you to write down a dollar amount of how much it would create for you. Quantify the contribution your dreams will have on your life.

5. **Write down three words that best describe how a positive outcome in your future feels.** Is it exciting? Invigorating? Thrilling? Is it pure bliss and joy? What is it? Write down three words that best describe how the future you just envisioned feels to you.

We increase our emotional intelligence every time we visualize our greatness. When we visualize or use our imagination to dream of a positive future, we are leaning into positive emotions deliberately. That's what you were doing when you imagined and wrote your answers to the questions above.

The choices we make in each moment are based on the things we value. We unconsciously evaluate what we value most of the time. We develop shortcuts to understand what's important to us and often we make choices based on what we think we value or what we valued in the past. Visualization is the simple act of setting aside a little time to deliberately dream of greatness, to re-evaluate and lay out some different choices on the table to pick from. When you do this, you are starting where you are and harnessing the power of your imagination to step up into your Zone of Greatness.

right action, right time

Rushing, pushing, and binging on action, ideas, and information creates so much frustration and pain we could easily avoid. If we take a moment to check in and start where we are right now, before we jump into action, it changes everything. Yet, we often ignore or feel like we don't have time and skip this step. Then we slip further into the Vicious Spin Cycle.

Often we may feel like our time just disappears and we can't get anything done. We create rules in our heads that dictate that we need to get some other things done before we can do the things we really want to do. But a lot of this chatter from our itty-bitty-shitty committee stems from overwhelm and frustration and could easily be managed differently. When we feel negatively emotionally charged, it is much more difficult to get stuff done, especially the stuff that's important to us—the things our feelings of greatness hinge on. Then we thrust ourselves into a downward spiral that can be very difficult to pull ourselves out of.

> If you're not getting the results that you want to get in life or business, if you feel like you are putting up with things or are feeling overwhelmed, it may be because you're pushing yourself to do the right thing at the wrong time or the wrong things at the wrong time.

When we feel like we are under the gun and we don't have a lot of time, that is not the right time to do big, creative thinking. For example, if one of the things that we want to do requires us to figure out something new and think big or if we feel overwhelmed (level 11 on the Emotional Thermometer), big thinking is not going to happen. Even if we do push ourselves to check off an item on our list or get a project completed, it won't be done very well. The quality won't be great. We will probably have to redo it, or worse yet, we will feel like we need to redo it but won't have time. Then we may carry the weight of that around with us often for months or years. We will have that lingering feeling of regret that we did not do great work. Sometimes it's valid, sometimes it's perfectionism, but we will never know because we didn't create the space to be great.

When we are feeling frustrated or discouraged, that's probably not a good time to do client work or something that we need to do for our business or career. Maybe that's a good time to get a quick win, like putting the laundry away so that we can create a feeling of accomplishment instead. That feeling of accomplishment will allow us to move up the Emotional Thermometer, and then we can tackle some of the more focused-driven projects or things that we might have been putting off.

If we wait until we are higher on the Emotional Thermometer, maybe until we are feeling hopeful, enthusiastic, or excited, that is the perfect time to focus on some big, creative thinking, important projects, and things that require a lot of attention.

When we start where we are and honor where we are, we don't need to push ourselves to do things. It's so much easier! In the last few chapters, you have learned some simple tools that you can use to move yourself up the Emotional Thermometer without pushing while you raise your emotional intelligence.

start where you are cheat sheet

By now, I hope you are beginning to realize that the way we feel has a major impact on our performance and productivity. You have begun to understand more about your emotional intelligence and have learned some tools to help you raise your EQ score.

Starting where you are is a critical step to getting into our Zone of Greatness. You have learned in this section that it works much better to start where you are and to do the right tasks at the right time and that taking your emotional temperature and celebrating your wins are tools that empower you to begin to nudge yourself lovingly into your Zone of Greatness.

Like me, you might not know how you feel at first. When I quit drinking. I had been an alcoholic for decades. I had numbed myself from my feelings, like a lot of us do. It might not be alcohol;

for you, it might be with TV, binging Netflix, or chocolate cake. Often when we don't enjoy how we feel, we find ways to numb ourselves—especially when we don't understand how we're feeling and our emotional EQ is low. When I quit drinking, I started asking myself, "How do I feel?" I had no way to answer the question. I felt lost. I wasn't in touch with how I was feeling. The Emotional Thermometer allowed me to get the hang of answering the question almost like a crutch so that I could learn how to walk again eventually without it.

There are a lot of different ways we could answer this question. The simplest and easiest way is to take our emotional temperature and acknowledge where we are in this moment. The more we do that, the more we begin to notice the nuances of where we are. We can begin to make connections and recognize triggers so that we can raise our EQ.

Just keep asking yourself, "Where am I right now?" and gradually start to notice. Recognize, anger, worry, blame, or discouragement. Then, as you get the hang of it, you will begin to discern and understand your emotions better. You may begin to see that what you thought was fear is actually excitement because they are very similar in how they present themselves in our bodies. Fear is almost exactly like excitement but without the breath. When you feel fear, sometimes it may be nudging you onto a different path. Other times, if you stop and take a breath, you will see that what you thought was fear was actually excitement letting you know you are already on the right path.

The question, "Where am I now?" allows us to start where we are and get a sense of how we're feeling so that we can do the right task at the right time, which is a game changer.

One of the key concepts we also learned in this section of the book is to get in the mood before we take action. This is especially important when we've been procrastinating or the action we want to take is pivotal to our forward momentum.

Procrastination is a pretty loaded word, but remember that procrastinating on something is just another way of saying "stuff you didn't do." Every time you catch yourself saying, "Oh, I've been procrastinating on that," just remind yourself "that's what I didn't do." No judgment.

When you don't feel like doing something and you are putting things off—"not doing stuff"—it's a good time to take your emotional temperature. Just take a moment and pause. Even the pause is going to help shift things. This will create the space for you to shift your emotional state. Think of it as emotional foreplay to really get you in the mood. And whenever possible, don't do anything unless you feel like doing it.

Now, I understand—there are some rules to this game of life that we're playing, and often we may be playing by someone else's rules. We may feel like we do not have complete freedom about what we do and when we do it. When I say don't do anything you don't feel like doing, it may feel absurd. Keep in mind, though, that when I say that it doesn't mean don't do it ever.

What I'm inviting you to do is acknowledge where you are before pushing yourself to do something you don't feel like doing. That pause may be enough to give you the clarity to see that there are actually other ways to approach the task at hand.

The pause may also allow you to realize that you can change how you feel. You can celebrate some wins or use your imagination to see a positive outcome to help you toward your Zone of Greatness.

I have created a series of cheat sheets for you to use to keep all the important concepts, questions, and tools you learn in each part of the book at your fingertips.

Download the Cheat Sheet for Greatness Habit One: Start Where You Are, as well as the other cheat sheets at **www.dailymomentumhub.com**

HABIT TWO

know what you want

"Tell me what you want, what you really, really want."
—Spice Girls

unstoppable

My Grandma Ada was an almost six-foot-tall powerhouse of a woman. Together with her husband, shortly after they were married, they built a house. Everybody pitched in and helped; because of that, they called the house "Friendship." It was the perfect name. The milkman would come over and have coffee at their table during his morning rounds. Every time I visited, there would be the window cleaner, the postman, or a local farmer sitting at the table with a cup of tea. Everybody was welcome. It truly was a house full of friendship.

After my grandfather passed away, my grandma moved into a flat close to my mum on the second floor of a small building in the village. She continued to be very sociable. She could go up and down the stairs several times daily with no problem. There was a superintendent who lived on the same floor who was right there, and my mum loved it because she could keep an eye on her.

And so, in her early eighties, Grandma Ada built a new life—a second chapter that she really enjoyed. And then she broke her hip. As it was healing, she was not able to get around as much. Even though friends and family would visit, she began to feel isolated. She couldn't go up and down the stairs whenever she wanted. This was not a situation that she enjoyed.

Her hip did heal very nicely, but the seed had been planted with what she did not want for herself, and what she did want began to blossom in her imagination. So, Grandma Ada started figuring out new options. She noticed some single-story bungalows that were down the street. There were no stairs in the bungalow, and each had a cute little garden in the back. She mentioned the bungalows to my mum who told her, "I think you're good where you are." Mum really enjoyed that the superintendent of the building was so close by, and it seemed like my grandma might be developing dementia just a little bit. My mum was worried that if my grandma moved, she wouldn't know where anything was, that it would be hard on both of them. Even though my mum did appreciate that it would be better for her to live in a one-level home, she felt it would be easier not to move my grandma.

But Grandma Ada stayed focused. She found out there was actually a bungalow available immediately. She even got an application form and filled it out all on her own. A few days later, she picked up the phone and called Mum and said, "I want you to do something with me today. I want you to come and look at that bungalow with me."

My mum told her, "Well, okay, but you know, I really don't think it's a good idea."

Later that day, they both went to the bungalow. After they looked around, my grandma and my mum stood in the kitchen. My grandma had the palm of her hand resting firmly, flat on the countertop. She looked at my mum and she said, "Well, what do you think?" My mum repeated her concerns: "I don't know. In your flat, you know where everything is. Moving could be confusing. And where you are, people are watching over you. I'm just not sure it's a good idea."

My grandma looked my mum dead in the eye. With her hand flat on the kitchen counter, she pounded down three times like a strong drum beat as she said emphatically, "I want it. I like it. And I am going to have it!" There was so much clarity, power, and strength in Grandma Ada in that moment that my mum couldn't say no.

And so, my grandma got exactly what she wanted. By the next month, she had moved into her bungalow with a little garden that brought her so much joy. Yes, she got confused and yes, she did have dementia, but she lived there happily for two years until she really couldn't be on her own anymore.

When we are clear about what we want, whether we are 42 or 82, just like Grandma Ada, we can do things that maybe we thought we couldn't. Once we have that kind of clarity and we've lined up what we want with a strong belief, we can have it, we are unstoppable.

one thing

It was a fall morning and the ladies and I were gathered over coffee for our Monthly Momentum meeting.

As we were finishing up, I gave the ladies their final instructions: "Everyone stand up and share your 'One Thing.'" I looked at our newest member, "Samantha, why don't you go first?"

Samantha stood up confidently. "I have two 'One Things,'" she announced. The room erupted in laughter. We all totally got it! Samantha didn't. She had tunnel vision and couldn't see the irony of her words. The "One Thing" concept, introduced by Gary Keller and Jay Papasan in their book, *The One Thing*, emphasizes the power of focusing on the single most important task that will make all other tasks simpler or even unnecessary, thereby enhancing productivity and effectiveness.

Multitasking is an addiction! We use it to prove ourselves, to attempt to deliver more, and to avoid saying "no." Multitasking is a surefire way to binge our way into burnout and overwhelm and avoid shining our greatness. When we are overwhelmed with activities, to-dos, and projects, there is no way we can look up, never mind see the great opportunities all around us. All we see is what's six inches in front of us, and who knows where we will end up.

If we want to soar up to greatness, we have to know what we want and prioritize it. We need to stop rationalizing loopholes, like the one Samantha found with her two One Things. In this section of the book, I will share tools to help you apply Greatness Habit Two: Know What You Want. Using the concept of the One Thing to avoid multitasking, we can prioritize and focus on what's important, stepping into our Zone of Greatness.

what's your one thing?

One of the big reasons that meditation works so well is that it forces a pause, a reboot. Meditation interrupts our thought patterns and allows us to rewire our mindset over time. Always knowing what your One Thing is works in much the same way.

My Daily 1 Thing is...

Just stopping to think about that question opens the door to creating space to be great. Honestly, the answer doesn't even matter as much as asking the question does. Keep asking it all the time. That way, we give ourselves little reboots all day long.

In the morning, what if you got up and asked, "What's my One Thing today?" It might be to work with a specific client, write an email, drop off a package at the post office, or have a really fun lunch with friends! Then, throughout the day, as you move from one segment of the day to another, ask again.

When we get up and start getting ready for the day, the One Thing might be, "I want to feel comfortable and confident." When we begin to make breakfast, it might be "to power up my energy." When we drive from one appointment to another, it might be "to learn something new as I listen to an audiobook."

The more we do this throughout the day, the more we reboot. Just remember to only have ONE One Thing at a time.

80/20

There is a concept known as Pareto's Rule, also called the 80/20 rule. This principle suggests that approximately 80% of effects arise from just 20% of the causes. For a practical example, consider a carpeted room in your home. While the carpet covers 100% of the room, you likely only walk on about 20% of it regularly. The remaining 80% sees much less use. This 80/20 rule can be applied to anything and is an effective tool for prioritization. It helps us identify the most impactful 20% of our actions or resources that create 80% of our results.

If we have a list of 100 people that we know, probably only 20 (or 20%) of them are really engaged and responsive to us on a regular basis. This is our inner circle of influence. These are the loyal people who show up and want to hang out with us and talk to us on a regular basis. The other 80 (80%) of them may be unresponsive, always busy, or don't tend to reach out to us very often.

Once we start noticing how the 80/20 principle is already true in our lives, then we can use that knowledge and apply it to anything. All we have to do is notice where our focus, attention, and energy are going and choose to focus on the top 20% instead of the full 100% of what is in front of us.

Now, if you are like me, the idea of doing calculations to figure out what is 20% and 80% can feel overwhelming. Don't worry—I'm going to make it super simple. Instead of doing all those calculations, we can use the One Thing concept we just learned in the last chapter. We can create a habit of looking at what is in front of us, which represents 100%, and then pick One Thing instead of doing it all.

Maybe make a list or a mind map to flush out all your ideas, and then ask yourself, "If I were to just put all of my energy, focus, and attention on One Thing, what would be the most impactful, important thing out of all these other things that I could focus on?"

When we concentrate on One Thing at a time, our focus is like sunlight on a magnifying glass when we hold it still; it catches things on fire. So often we are busy with so many projects, to-dos, and commitments, it's like we keep moving the magnifying glass around and it never catches anything on fire.

If that sounds familiar, you are going to be amazed at what happens to your ability to focus and finish things when you shift to prioritizing using the One Thing rather than making an ordered to-do list or trying to do everything.

Multi-tasking as a success tool is a myth. Now, I'm going to give you a warning here: if you have been a multi-tasking ninja for a while, when you begin to shift into focusing on One Thing at a time, it's going to feel a little bit scary and under-productive. You may not be able to do all that you feel like you have to do. But trust me, if you find your One Thing and you zero in on it, it's going to create some serious momentum for you!

You may need to develop a little faith around the One Thing concept first until your own experience gives you enough evidence to trust it. However, when you really dive into the One Thing mindset, you're going to see incredible results from your actions, your activity, and your focus.

As a coach, it is common for me to assign homework at the end of a session with clients. I had fallen into a habit of asking clients to do three things, and typically, clients did none of them at all! What I noticed was that, for most clients, having three things to do was distracting and overwhelming. They easily forgot what they were supposed to do, even though we had come up with the homework together and I had emailed it to them. In my gut, I really just wanted to give them One Thing to do, but I thought that would slow down their progress or perhaps they would see less value in working with me.

Then one day, one of my members gave me the most wonderful Valentine's gift: *The One Thing* by Gary Keller. The book gave me the permission I needed to have my clients focus on just One Thing.

It also gave me the faith I needed to back up my gut instinct that focusing on One Thing is a much more effective and productive way to seize your greatness than anything else.

At this point in our journey, it is time to walk your talk! I want you to take a moment to think about how to apply the 80/20 rule and the One Thing to your life right now. What could you do right now that would make the most impact in your professional or personal life? Don't skip this step!

Don't slip into perfection mode and go off the rails and disappear down a black hole. Just give yourself the space and time, maybe 15 minutes and a walk around the block. Ask yourself, "What is the One Thing, if I committed to it no matter what, that would sky-rocket me to achieve greatness in the areas that are truly important to me?"

And here's the most important part: open yourself up to receive the answer! And when it comes, don't judge it; instead, commit to using it as your guide for the rest of this book. Can you do that? If you can, you are well on your way to greatness.

So often I hear women sharing that they have no time. Yes, you may not have enough time to do everything (or 100%), but if you choose to focus on One Thing (or 20%), you will master your time, upgrade your actions, and increase your energy! The truth is, it's not that we have too little time to do the things we need to do, it's that we feel an addiction or need to do too many things. When we multi-task, we're not getting more done; we are wasting our time, money, and energy. When everything is important, nothing is really important. It's an unwinnable cycle of doing that is exhausting.

Choosing One Thing is not choosing two or three important things. To focus on three things is multi-tasking. To focus on One Thing is to be great. Today, we often feel an obligation or a compulsion to multi-task. Sometimes multi-tasking means literally doing multiple things at once, which incidentally is impossible, but more about that in a minute. And sometimes multi-tasking means having several projects cooking at the same time that are equally important. It is very hard to know what is a priority if everything feels equally important. Multi-tasking pulls us in a million different directions at once. To define a One Thing is to choose something as the most important, to direct most of our energy to it, and to allow it to expand, grow, and move us forward.

So, let's take a look at how to implement the One Thing tool. I think you will find it creates a little more flexibility than you first imagined. To start, you may simply take it day by day or project by project. You can ask, "What is my One Thing for today?" This is a key part of the Daily Momentum process, and I will break it down in even more detail later in the book.

Remember when we choose our One Thing, it should be the thing that feels like the 20%—the action, project, or to-do that will create the most impact. How do we know? Sometimes we know from experience. We can look back at what has worked in the past. We can also simply use our inner guidance system. Tune into how we feel and notice if one project or idea feels lighter, fun, or easier than the others. More than likely, our One Thing will feel like the easiest and most fun path forward to greatness.

What's nice about this is that when we ask ourselves, "What is my One Thing?", we give ourselves a little reboot. I don't know about you, but I go down rabbit holes sometimes throughout the day. I get on the computer to follow up with someone in my contact management software, and then the next thing I know, I'm watching videos of all the new updates in the software and I've completely forgotten what I was doing to begin with. It's like opening the fridge to get the milk for your coffee and getting distracted by the muffins and forgetting what you went to the fridge for to start with. Asking, "What is my One Thing?" brings you back to the present moment.

We function best when we are taking time throughout the day and cultivating the habit of checking in with ourselves and asking, "What's my One Thing right now?" We can even create a little mantra, a pattern interrupt on a post-it note, or a reminder on our watch. Throughout the day, simply pausing, taking a breath, and checking in with, "What is my One Thing right now?" can reconnect us with what's important, minimize distractions, and breathe life and energy into our actions.

Asking ourselves this simple question builds on the "What do I want?" question I introduced earlier in the book. It is a reminder that we are human with five senses working overtime. It creates a disruption of our auto-pilot mode, reminding us that we can instead operate from a place of choice.

When we focus on One Thing at a time, we create a lot of momentum. On the other hand, when we focus on a lot of different things seemingly at the same time, it slows us down. What we are doing is just jumping around really quickly and losing a lot of momentum with each jump from task to task.

What if every day, you spent as little as 15 minutes on your One Thing? What momentum might that create for you? The results may very well blow you away. They may even be great! That's the power of focus.

right now

If we really want to break away from busyness and burnout and shift from good to great, then knowing how to focus is essential. As you have learned already, when we concentrate our energy and attention, we can harness the full power of our *unstoppableness*, just like Grandma Ada. We can use the One Thing tool to help us get clear and focused, but what about all the other projects and tasks on our plate that aren't our One Thing? What about when we feel confused and maybe don't even know what we want? What if we can't figure out our One Thing?

The Right Now Worksheet is a simple tool we can pull out at any time to help us shift into our Zone of Greatness. It is a valuable tool for those moments when we're feeling overwhelmed, lost, or in need of clarity, and it is incredibly useful at the start of each day.

The Right Now question prompts are an important piece of Daily Momentum, and you will be answering them each day as you begin your Daily Momentum practice. I will go over the Daily Momentum process step by step for you later in the book. For now, the questions from the Right Now Worksheet can serve as excellent journal prompts to use anytime to help you clear your mind and articulate your thoughts on paper.

When we are feeling a little bit low on the Emotional Thermometer and we want to nudge our way up, the Right Now Worksheet can often quickly move us into another emotional state. If you want to figure out how to stay in your Zone of Greatness, then this tool is going to help you do just that. It's like a "greatness intervention" that we can activate for ourselves, anytime we choose. We don't have to be on the lower end of the Emotional Thermometer to tap into its power either; we can use this tool to lift us even higher up the scale and create more joy and fun on an already great day too.

It's best to use the Right Now Worksheet with no goal, desire, or agenda in mind. This tool is not about helping you create a specific result. Instead, the Right Now Worksheet is a way to check in, activate your curiosity, open you up to new ideas, or wake you up to where you are right now. And it is a fabulous way to stumble across what you want and ideas for your One Thing. Just don't go seeking them out; let them come to you as you answer the series of prompts in the worksheet.

EXERCISE | THE RIGHT NOW WORKSHEET

The Right Now Worksheet is a series of writing prompts. It gives you the beginning of a sentence to complete on several different themes. This technique gets you out of your head and into your heart and is similar to journaling but in a short, simple format that can be quicker and more effective.

Right now, I feel...

We can get into a comfortable rut of using a very small emotional vocabulary if we don't deliberately stretch ourselves. As a productivity coach, I love that I get to work with men and women who are innovative. And yet, when I ask them, "How are you doing?", or, "How do you feel right now?", their response is usually "good" or "fine." These are the go-to four-letter words I want you to avoid. Instead of relying on these go-to words, if we challenge ourselves, we can tune in to the nuances of how we really feel and learn how to communicate and understand our emotions better.

When we have to pause to think, "How do I feel right now?", it causes a pattern interruption. It's an opportunity for us to look within and take our emotional temperature, and if we don't like what we find, we can change it. Go-to-words, spoken unconsciously out of habit, deny us this amazing opportunity for growth. The invitation to respond to the prompt, "Right now, I feel..." is a chance to experiment with upgrading our emotional vocabulary.

At first, you might be at a loss for words, but that's okay; you can glance over the Emotional Thermometer I shared with you earlier for inspiration. Just remember, anything is better than just "good" or "fine."

Are you feeling spunky? I love that word from the '80s. Are you feeling supported? Are you feeling supreme? Maybe you are feeling frugal or fun. Perhaps right now you feel brave, amused, or appreciated. The objective here is not to sugarcoat things. We are on a quest for truth. This is a truth that can absolutely set you free!

The next thing I'm going to do right now is...

The next prompt invites us to place ourselves in the present moment. It creates a pause between actions or activities to notice what we have been doing and what we are going to do next. Once again, this creates a pattern interruption. Perhaps our response is, "I'm going to eat lunch," or, "I'm going to sit down and turn on the computer," or, "I'm going for a walk." This prompt gives us a moment to find the context of where we are in the day.

Right now, I want...

From the first pages of our journey together, I have been inviting you to explore what it is you want, to ignite your hunger, define your passion, and explore what feels satisfying. When we answer, "Right now, I want...", we can be big and decadent if we like. However, most of the time, simple "wants" will jump into our minds, things that we perhaps didn't even realize we wanted. And often our "wants" can easily be delivered just because we pause to ask ourselves, "Right now, I want...".

Give yourself full permission to answer this prompt. You are not required to act on it or achieve it. Your only responsibility is to answer the prompt and learn a little bit more about yourself, at this moment. As you do this, you create new choice points as possibilities in your future. You are creating a playlist of fun ideas, adventures, and information that you can download and pick from any time you like.

What do you want right now? A vacation in Hawaii? A piece of chocolate? Don't limit yourself to one want—write down as many as you like. Perhaps you want clarity, progress, or inspiration. Maybe you want more joy right now or ease. Sometimes it will be environmental: "I want to feel cooler," "more comfortable," or "less noisy."

Be honest with yourself, not realistic. This is not the time to limit yourself to the constraints of your current reality. Even if you want a ten-day vacation in Hawaii and you've already got a jam-packed week, allow yourself to want the vacation. Acknowledge it. Plant the seeds; you don't know what might grow in the future if you do. And because you have acknowledged the desire for a ten-day vacation in Hawaii, maybe it will shift how you show up this week. Perhaps you will make different choices just because you gave yourself permission to ask and answer this prompt truthfully. Maybe you will sit in the sun for a few minutes at lunchtime, glance over some travel websites, or ask your best friend if she would like to go to Hawaii.

Right now, I appreciate...

What do you appreciate right now? What are you grateful for? As I write this, I appreciate:

- my beautiful patio

- my strong husband who will chop things down and get all scratched up and bloody to allow me to appreciate my bougainvillea

- my new pergola

- a lovely cup of coffee in the morning

- my journal

- the amazing women who are members of the Momentum Squad

- technology and Zoom and my team for creating my slide deck

- And right now, I appreciate how easy it is for us all to connect in the world, from anywhere

Notice how detailed and specific I'm being. The more clearly we identify the things we appreciate, the more real they feel. When we are broad and general and instead say, "I appreciate my husband, my backyard, my community, or my family," we don't feel the same degree of appreciation; it's not as powerful. I'm not saying there's anything wrong with appreciating things in a broad and general way, but when we are specific about exactly what we're appreciating, that specificity seems to intensify our feelings of appreciation even more. So, milk it!

And keep in mind that we can't appreciate something and feel negative emotions like shame, guilt, or fear at the same time. Appreciation is a great way to shift yourself into your Zone of Greatness.

Right now, I'm having lots of fun...

What is fun in your world right now? As I write this, I'm having lots of fun because it's my favorite time of the year playing in the pool.

- Right now, I'm having lots of fun laying in my hammock

- Right now, I'm having lots of fun hanging out on my patio

- Right now, I'm having lots of fun writing

- Right now, I'm having lots of fun making every day feel like a vacation

As you answer this prompt, you may find repetition of some of the things you have already mentioned with the other prompts. That's okay; when we repeat ourselves, we anchor in and affirm more of what we want. We build a solid foundation to create more fun stuff to be grateful for.

It may have been a while since you stopped to think about what's fun. If so, this prompt may stump you at first. Take your time and enjoy becoming curious again about your needs, desires, and wants. If we are not clear on what is fun, then it's very hard to find more of it. As we fine-tune our palate to more fun and realize what fun really means to us, we will magically find more of those fun things showing up in our future.

Right now, I want to eat/drink...

Our bodies, not just our brains, are pretty smart. They can inform us of exactly how to take care of them if we listen. Just like speaking a new language, it may feel like it's hard to hear what our body wants at first. We may find ourselves noticing that our body needs something but we can't figure out what, so we eat everything in sight without feeling satiated, only to realize a few minutes later that we are thirsty. At first, a craving or desire will not be as clear as it can be. Ask questions to get clearer, like, "Is it salt I am craving or sugar?"

We may have deprived or starved ourselves of certain substances, and so at first, until our body is satisfied, we may need to simply fill ourselves up again. Perhaps we feel a desire to eat chocolate cake, but once we have given ourselves permission, if we continue to listen, we may feel that desire satiated after just a few bites. This is the concept behind intentional eating. When we listen, we can actually eat whatever we want and regulate ourselves rather than starving and depriving ourselves.

It's interesting that pretty much every time I ask myself, "What do I want to eat/drink right now?" water is always right up there at the top. I may even stop the Right Now Worksheet, grab a big chug of water to satisfy my thirst, and then ask the question again. As we fulfill a desire, we will often find other desires underneath. Desires are like layers we can keep diving deeper into.

This prompt around food and drink may eventually unleash your sense of adventure. Perhaps you will find yourself experimenting with new and different flavors or flavor combinations, experimenting with new things, and getting to know what you like best.

Right now, my body is enjoying the flavor of fresh mint. I have a mint patch in my garden, and I came across a recipe for a drink that includes muddled mint, pomegranate molasses, and sparkling water. If I wasn't getting curious and listening to my body, I would probably not have been bothered to go to all that trouble. Clarity gets us into momentum.

This idea of following your body's prompts may scare you, especially if you have struggled with addiction before, as I have. When I felt the desire to drink in the past, it was an unconscious habit that was masking many other needs. If you feel compelled to eat and drink substances that are doing you harm, you will first want to detox yourself from the addiction. The idea of intuitive eating and following your body's lead only works when you are conscious in your body. When I was in addiction for two decades, I was not living consciously and therefore not able to hear the true needs and desires of my body. It wasn't till I quit that I was able to really listen to my body.

There are times when I want to eat and drink food that is full of vegetables and feels nutritious and clean and other times when I want chocolate brownies or fries. Can you have faith in following or at least listening to the prompts your body gives you when you take the time to ask and listen to what it wants? Even if it is something that you have chosen to label in your mind as unhealthy, when we really listen, we can also notice the little impulses to stop when we have had enough.

Right now, it would be great if...

Now it's time to unleash our imaginations. With this prompt, we can daydream and explore what we can create. Imagine you have a magic wand. Think outside the box. This prompt is designed to get us thinking beyond "what is" right now. I know it is a little contradictory, but you get it, right?

- Right now, it would be great if I could figure out the perfect place to go on vacation

- Right now, it would be great if I could figure out how to get the team aligned with some of the new tools.

- Right now, it would be great if I had more guidance about the next steps to take and in which order

- Right now, it would be great if I had less to do

Right Now, I am Looking Forward to...

What are you looking forward to? We can use this prompt to dream about things we know we will be doing in the future and feed the excitement to fuel us today. This prompt can also highlight our frustration with our present moment. If we feel tired and burned out and time is scarce, we may find ourselves writing our way out of those feelings on the page. You might be looking forward to more of something like time, money, or space. When we are as specific as we can be, we plant seeds that can take root.

Broad and general statements like "more time" are generally not as powerful as "more time to go on vacation with family." Quite often I find myself craving more clarity, direction, or information in the future. Therefore, when I prompt myself with, "Right now, I'm looking forward to...", I find myself focusing on more general intangibles at first. That is not a problem; just answering the prompt several times, moving through the layers, will begin to point you more specifically toward what you want.

- Right now, I'm looking forward to dipping in the pool

- Right now, I'm looking forward to my bulletproof coffee

- Right now, I am looking forward to figuring out how I can get together in person and organize our next retreat

- Right now, I'm looking forward to things falling into place

- Right now, I'm looking forward to learning everything I need about launching a new product

- Right now, I'm looking forward to having more time for family

- Right now, I'm looking forward to spending more time

with girlfriends and having fun

Right now, the question I'm asking is...

By now, you can see how powerful questions are. By challenging yourself to always be asking a question, you are keeping the fire of curiosity lit. Many decades ago, a series of books by James Redfield called *The Celestine Prophecy* introduced several personal development ideas in a narrative form. One of the premises in the books centered on always knowing what your question is and moving from one question to the next as your question is answered. The concept was similar to the idea of a treasure hunt, but instead of finding physical clues, the clues came in the form of answers to your questions delivered from different people, places, and things you encountered along your journey. The Right Now Worksheet prompt, "The question I am asking right now is...." invites you to play the question treasure hunt game too.

If we are feeling off or looking for a boost, a question can be a great next action step, a jumping-off point into possibilities available at your fingertips. Anytime we feel unsettled or are struggling to focus, we can quickly and easily harness our attention and enjoy more clarity and focus by finding a question.

If we are looking for something but maybe haven't pinpointed exactly what that something is, a question can point us in the right direction. We can use questions, like Goldilocks, to discern what we do and don't want. We might start with a statement about what we do or don't want and then turn it into a question. Suddenly, instead of a dead end, we magically created a door! Questions are jumping-off points that allow us to shift out of being immersed in the problem and into new possibilities.

Just getting curious about a challenge or problem will ease things and move us up the Emotional Thermometer. A question sets a positive expectation that can move us forward very quickly if we are ready.

Bring it All Together

I recommend you download the Right Now Worksheet and put it on a clipboard so that you can grab it anytime and use it. Write in pencil or purchase a laminated version from the online store at www.thegetitdonesystem.com.

In just five minutes, you can work your way through this worksheet anytime you need it. The order of the prompts on the Right Now Worksheet is important. The previous prompts are designed to move you into conscious contemplation and prime you for the next. Each time you use the Right Now Worksheet, you can look forward to more clarity, more direction, more focus, and, of course, more greatness. If you take a moment to use this tool before you get into action, it will change what you do, when you do it, and even how you do it, so you can step into projects, activities, and experiences fully aware. This simple tool could change the trajectory of your day, week, and (not to be dramatic) your life.

know what you want cheat sheet

For over a decade, I wanted to write a best-selling book. I wasn't clear on the topic, and the project felt big and hard, mainly because I felt like it had to be perfect. So, what did I do? I sat back and waited for that perfect "a-ha" idea to come to me. But I didn't create the space for it to show up. And guess what? Nothing showed up.

If somebody had asked me, "What do you want?", I could have answered. I would have said, "I want to take all the knowledge I have and be a best-selling author." On the surface, it might have seemed like I knew what I wanted, but if you really watched me, you would see that I didn't know what I wanted because actions speak louder than words. I wasn't doing anything to move toward becoming a best-selling author, not even stopping to listen for an impulse of what to do.

My biggest challenge was that I wasn't clear on exactly what the "perfect" topic was for that number one best-selling book I had inside me. My ideas all felt vague and uninspiring.

If you ever find yourself in a position where you think you know what you want and nothing's happening, then experiment with asking yourself, "Do I really know what I want? What do I want?", and then stop and listen deeply.

Can you think back to the last experience you had of really knowing something? Knowing something conclusively and certainly with your whole being? When we know something in such a deep way that it just feels like truth, things click into place. Clarity is the best word I have found to most accurately describe the kind of focus we have when we know what we want and are in our Zone of Greatness. Clarity is the magical ingredient that can jump-start our desire and turn it into momentum. Clarity is the easiest, quickest way I know to get focused and into action. Clarity is knowing what you want!

One day, I sat watching my daughter, Sofie, in her gymnastics class, and I was staring off into space. No thoughts. No busyness. No to-do list. And out of nowhere, like it had been waiting all this time for a place to land, the perfect title for the book I wanted to write popped right into my head. It just showed up when I wasn't even "trying." I grabbed some paper, and I did a mind map with the title in the middle of the page, then I outlined the content for each of the chapters. Each idea came to mind like little thought bubbles. I put them all on the page. I like to think of this process as catching raindrops. All you really need to do is grab an empty bucket and stand in the rain. That day, my empty mind and the blank page were the bucket and the rain was the thoughts I created the space to receive.

About thirty minutes later, on that piece of paper were all the main ideas I wanted to include in my new book, all organized perfectly together. Before, they had just been a confusing, overwhelming jumble of ideas in my head, tangled up with other people's needs and things I needed to do. And in just moments, they were beautifully and compellingly organized on the page in my messy handwriting. Within two weeks, I had written *The Get it Done Diva's Guide to Business* and published it, with it hitting number one on Amazon in three different categories.

Most of the time, when we are not doing the stuff that we want to get done, it's probably not laziness. When we find ourselves procrastinating or feeling overwhelmed, it's likely because we are not 100% clear about what we want.

When you catch yourself not doing something that you know you want to do, remember the P-word. Take your emotional temperature. How are you feeling? Use the Right Now Worksheet to refocus. Ten minutes is all it takes. Just ten minutes can cut through any distractions like a knife and laser-focus your attention to get you back into your Zone of Greatness.

Download the cheat sheet for Greatness Habit Two: Know What You Want as well as The Right Now Worksheet at www.dailymomentumhub.com

Now that you are beginning to understand the Greatness Habit Two: Know What You Want, isn't it exciting to realize your full power? If we really want to, we can do anything. When we let go of our resistance and allow ourselves to ask, "What do I want?" we can focus so deeply, we can move mountains. I want you to BE moved. That is what it feels like to be in momentum. It's jumping on and riding that wave and letting the energy below it, the tide, do all the work. And this is why I continue to keep challenging you. If you are not moving forward in the way you would like, it may very well simply be that you don't know exactly what you want.

HABIT THREE

make tomorrow better than today

"It's a new dawn, it's a new day, it's a new life, for me, and I'm feeling good."

—Nina Simone

wings

My mum stood, looking at me with frustration and despair. "Why can't you have a regular wedding like everyone else?"

You see, I wanted a Faire and Goblin-themed wedding. Yes, that's faire with an *e*, not a *y*; not a cute Disney production. Think more along the lines of *The Lord of the Rings* meets *The Princess Bride*. Picture mischievous goblins running through the forest and fairies with wings made of woodland branches and dew drops. I know, it's a little weird—okay, maybe a lot. But I was 32 years old, and I was crystal clear that I wanted a faire wedding, much to my mum's despair!

Everyone in the wedding party was wearing wings. The groomsmen wore black-feathered wings over their tuxedos, and the bridal party wore full-length, iridescent dragonfly wings. Everyone had said a big YES to wings, sacrificing their dignity and taking a leap of faith in my faire and goblin vision—everyone except my dad. He didn't tell me no directly, but when he got wind of the whole wing thing, he told my stepmum, "No, absolutely not. I'm not wearing wings!"

Wings! Maybe they are not for everyone. Look at the caterpillar; it goes along quite happily with its life, wing-free. That is until one day, it changes its mind. It creates a cocoon, dissolves into goo, and slowly sprouts new limbs and wings. Then life gives it a little nudge, and it scrambles its way out of its cocoon, spreads its wings, and launches itself into a new life.

I know a lot about cocoons! By the time I was 19 years old, I had built myself a pretty good one. After struggling with addiction and depression for years, I just felt completely hopeless. Then one day on my way to work, I sat at the back of a bus and overdosed on pain pills. As I slipped into unconsciousness, I felt a nudge to change my mind and fight my way out of my cocoon. I reached beyond all the pain and shame and admitted to the stranger in front of me what I had done. Minutes later, I was in the hospital with tubes down my throat, being given a second chance.

It's not always easy to make tomorrow better than today. I had to admit I was wrong, ask for help, shift my behavior and beliefs, and let go of conclusions I had made about myself in order to embrace a new tomorrow.

But because of that second chance, here I was, ready to give my hand to the king of the goblins, barefoot in a woody clearing, with a bubble machine at the ready.

Twenty minutes before the wedding ceremony, my mum stood, reluctantly, holding a four-foot span of pussy willow branches tied together with ribbon and glue-gunned jewels. "How are you going to attach them?" "What about tying them onto the straps of your wedding dress?" my friend Chino suggested. There I stood, looking out of the window as my mum and Chino gave me wings, ready to launch into my new life!

As the pre-ceremony music began, I strode down the hallway, and when I turned the corner into the living room, there, standing in his black-feathered wings, was my dad. "You changed your mind," I said, beaming. He nodded, smiled, and took my arm to walk me down the aisle.

Since my fairie and goblin wedding day, I have moved, changed jobs, started my own business, and given up drinking. Every one of those pivotal life events was made possible because life nudged me to make tomorrow better than today. And I listened. I found the courage to shift a behavior, belief, or decision I had previously made. I changed my mind and chose something different instead.

Is life nudging you to make tomorrow better than today and step into even more greatness? Is there an area of your life where you are digging in your heels to keep things as they are when it's time for change? What if instead you found the courage to change your mind, give yourself a second chance, or do something completely different today to make a better tomorrow? In the next part of the book, we dive into Greatness Habit Three: Make Tomorrow Better

Than Today. I will give you tools to help you disrupt your current reality, embrace change, and create upgrades to step even more into your greatness and create a habit of always making tomorrow better than today.

change

Change is the only constant in life. We can embrace it, we can fight it or, if we choose to, we can harness the power of change and use it to step into greatness.

What is change?
Change is when things are different than they were before.
Change is to break out of a regular habit or routine or even
to shift our entire life. When we move, get married, or start a
new job, we throw ourselves into change. Change always feels
uncomfortable at first, and it often seems like it happens to us
rather than through us. But it doesn't have to be that way.

We spend a lot of our lives adapting to and navigating change in varying degrees. Change can look like an upgrade to what already is, reinventing it completely, or letting something go.

After I chose to stop drinking and freed myself from addiction, I had changed, but the people around me were not yet up to speed with the change. Often this can be one of the hardest parts of change: learning how to interact with your old life, as the new you. I struggled with how to define myself. What do I tell friends and family when they offer me a drink? How do I navigate this? I found myself really struggling and stressing about what to say. Then my brilliant husband came to my rescue with a short little sentence that said it perfectly. When someone asked me, "Why aren't you drinking?", instead of needing to explain myself, I could simply say, "This is really working for me right now." Within these eight words lay freedom, clarity, and the answer I had been looking for to help me step into my tomorrow.

Change can feel overwhelming enough; sometimes we don't need to pin ourselves down to it too soon. By stating these eight words, I could feel the freedom to just be where I was in that moment, in the embryo of change, without needing to pin myself down to one label. This is especially helpful when you are in the beginning stages of change, which you will find more of now that you have stepped out on a path from good to great.

As we begin to embrace more change, it helps if we surround ourselves with a winning social environment and find people who won't push or aggravate the change that is evolving within us—people who, like my wonderful husband, will let you figure it out on your own and spread your wings to fly or crash. People who will pick you back up and help you launch off again without judgment. People who will allow you to forge your own path.

As you explore this habit of greatness, please resist the impulse to get into "doing," "fixing," or even "pushing" yourself to make tomorrow better than today. Instead, ask questions to spark new ideas and open yourself up to new possibilities and choices. Be careful not to push change—and, in doing so, create more guilt, overwhelm, and burnout. When any new insights show up, greet them from a place of, "Hmm, isn't that interesting?" rather than creating a whole bunch of new things to do or "shoulds." That's the old, good you, not the great version running the show.

The tools in this book invite you to create positive change without all that "trying." Instead, you can tap into your natural curiosity, using questions to create change gently and easily, without pushing. Just ask questions and see what happens. Asking questions to activate our natural sense of curiosity allows changes to happen easily. This results in not only an increase in productivity, but we also feel more satisfied at the end of each day. I am going to show you how to do that in the next few chapters.

We will always be evolving, so it is time to embrace the uncertainty, uncomfortableness, and excitement of change! There are three key approaches to change: to reboot (or start over), to deliberately disrupt your reality (to create change on purpose), and to upgrade (choose to improve your reality). In this section, you will find tools and ideas to help you explore all three of these approaches. So, get ready, because it's time to get uncomfortable. It's time to embrace change.

jet lag

One of my favorite ways to create change via a reboot is jet lag. When I get home from traveling across different time zones, jet lag throws my body into chaos as I move from one time zone to another. Massive change is why being on vacation can feel so good or maybe scary. When we take ourselves out of our usual routine and environment, we deliberately disrupt our reality. On vacation, so many things change, including our sense of time. This allows seemingly regular activities to feel fresh and new, both on vacation and even when we arrive home before we start to acclimatize again. It may feel uncomfortable when our lives are deliberately disrupted like this, but we are usually much more present in these circumstances and more open to understanding what we want than at any other time.

When I travel back from England to my home in the United States, I don't usually feel the effects of a jet lag reboot until the morning after I arrive home. Typically, I travel all day, go to bed exhausted, and sleep exceptionally well. Then my reboot takes full effect the next morning. For me, it always feels easy and natural to be up earlier after a trip to England. That magical morning, everything feels new. Being a morning person, I love this.

I notice myself being more curious and asking more questions. Do I want to get up? At what time? Do I want to get up earlier? What do I want to do when I get up? What do I want to eat for breakfast? Suddenly, all these little seemingly mundane details that made up my previous life are all shaken up, and to me, it is bliss!

Having jet lag is an opportunity to question everything. It is a chance to create something new, to create change, and to start over. The jet lag reboot shakes up all the routines that I had before. I invite this to happen by not slipping back into my regular routines right away. I build in a buffer of time after a trip for this specific purpose because I know if I create the space, changes will present themselves to me in this special time. I listen deeply to what my body is telling me. I explore how to do things differently, open myself up to what feels good, and take full advantage of being in this state of change.

curiosity

To be curious is to enquire, listen, lean in, and ask questions. Questions are one of the most powerful ways to explore change so that we can look at how to make tomorrow better than today. It always amazes me how a short, simple question can change everything in seconds. A question can invite you to change your opinion, take action, or move you from overwhelm to excitement. A question is like a laser; it works in seconds and cuts right to the core. Questions can wake you up and open up new options, ideas, inspiration, and possibilities. They can also give you a reality check and show you clearly what is not working, allowing you to face the facts and choose differently.

My best friend Jessica is a powerful question-asker. One time, as I was pondering what to do next with the membership community I run, she asked me:

"Do you want to continue doing this?"

"Is this working for everybody?"

"Why have a membership?"

"What's in it for you?"

For me? I was so used to looking at what membership was for my members, not me. These questions invited me to look at things from an entirely different perspective. That question alone has inspired me to shape and create different products and services. I continue to lead the members of the Momentum Squad after almost two decades without getting burned out or bored. A simple question enabled me to bring excitement and greatness to the community, and it still does.

Not all questions are created equally. Leading or insincere questions, asked without a true desire for an answer, are not what I am talking about here. Instead, I am focused on open-ended questions, which are like a door inviting us to explore and discover more about ourselves and other people. Usually, the best questions are the simplest—questions like, "What do you want?", and, "What are you looking forward to?" These are simple, open questions that challenge us to think beyond now and into what's next. They move us out of the problem and into solution thinking. Let's explore that a little more in the next chapter.

solution thinking

For decades, I wanted to quit drinking. I knew clearly what I didn't want, but I still couldn't find a path to lead me out of my addiction.

I didn't realize until later that it was because I was focusing on what I didn't want at the time, not what I wanted. I was marinating in the problem. I felt stuck. Then there was a moment that honestly felt like divine intervention. In that moment, I clearly saw that I was stuck in a loop of desperately looking for an answer, but I hadn't taken the time to ask the most important question: what did I want? Like many people, I was obsessing over finding answers, oblivious to the fact that, just like a lock needs a key, an answer needs a question.

When I realized the conundrum I had created for myself, I instantly shifted my energy into solution thinking instead. Just the simple act of acknowledging that I was feeling stuck in the problem moved me out of the problem and into the solution in a split second.

Once we get good at noticing how we are feeling and asking questions by using the Right Now Worksheet, we can move into solution thinking much quicker, sometimes before we even clearly formulate a question. Just the desire to understand what the question might be is enough.

Think of it like when we move from a warm to a cold room. We notice the shift in temperature; we just feel it. We can train ourselves to notice how the energy of solution feels versus the energy we feel when we are stuck in a problem. Now, I know this all might feel a little out there, but bear with me. I am not asking you to have blind faith here; instead, play with the two different feelings of stuck and solution yourself.

Albert Einstein is quoted as saying, "We cannot solve our problems with the same thinking that we used when we created them." Einstein leveraged solution thinking to uncover many mathematical equations, so why not see if you can tap into it too?

You can use a tool we already learned—the Emotional Thermometer. When we feel stuck in a problem, we may feel scared and afraid. When we are living in fear, we are not in the lower end of the Emotional Thermometer. And you guessed it—being in the energy of solution will feel like the upper-end of the scale. When we are excited and anticipating what's coming next, we are expanding our imagination and living on the upper-end of the Emotional Thermometer. So now, as you start to notice where you are on the scale, you can also identify if you are in the energy of a problem or a solution.

Everything that we have ever created was born out of a question. I want you to sit with that for a minute because it's a pretty powerful statement. Everything is born out of the energy of a question because the energy of a question is the energy of creation.

Think about something new or different in your life. Maybe you just started a new business, began a new relationship, or got a new car. It doesn't have to be something big. Maybe you had your hair cut in a new way, took a new route to work, or tried a new dinner recipe. It doesn't matter what it is; everything new begins with a question.

The question might have been, "How can I do this better?" Maybe because something wasn't working in your job, your business, or your relationship. And that "problem" moved into a solution the minute you asked a question.

- How can I do this better?

- How can I make more money doing this?

- What would it take for me to work from home?

- Who is the perfect mate?

These questions are the types of questions that are the catalyst for change.

You might be right smack bang in the middle of a question in your life right now and not even realize it. When we ask a question, it challenges us to think differently. Questions move us out of being stuck. When we ask a question like, "How can I make this work better?", we have to look forward, we have to look beyond today and focus on a better tomorrow.

When we feel stuck or impatient and all we are doing is looking at what is and where we are right now without asking a question, we cannot move forward. We cannot move beyond our problems into solution thinking. All we are doing is digging a deeper hole of stuckness.

If we are not asking a question, we are in the problem. When we are explaining and telling the story of why we are where we are right now, that's just sitting and marinating in the problem. Usually, we don't want to stay there for very long because it doesn't feel good. All sitting, festering, scratching, and aggravating the problem does is create more stuckness and frustration. Earlier, when I introduced you to Greatness Habit One: Start Where You Are, you might have noticed we didn't get into figuring out why you were where you are. That would have moved you down the Emotional Thermometer. We just focused on where you were.

What if every time you feel stuck, instead of going to that natural place of explaining yourself, you choose not to tell the story of where you are and how you got there? Don't complain or dig your heels in; instead, ask a question and activate solution thinking.

21 Questions

I have come up with 21 questions that you can use when you feel like you want to deliberately disrupt your reality, get unstuck, reboot, or upgrade any area of your life.

You can download all 21 questions and learn more about them at www.dailymomentumhub.com

Anytime you ask a question, don't push for answers. The magic is simply in asking the question and then stepping away. Give yourself the space to receive the answer. You might take a question on a walk with you and just let it simmer as you're walking.

daily debrief

Now that you can see how powerful a question can be, I am going to introduce you to two questions you will be answering at the end of every day as part of your Daily Debrief.

Remember the Emotional Thermometer from the Start Where You Are Habit of Greatness section of the book? This simple tool is a list of 22 words to help you identify how you are feeling at any given moment. At the bottom of the scale sits fear. Further up you will find anger, doubt, and overwhelm. At the top end of the scale, you will find joy, appreciation, and passion. And right between words seven and eight, you will find the sweet spot: satisfaction, or you might think of it as contentment. Satisfaction is the turning point where you shift from good to great.

Most people are pretty good at identifying what satisfaction feels like, so we can streamline the entire emotional scale into just two states to make it even simpler. We are either feeling satisfied (at seven

or higher on the Emotional Thermometer) or we are feeling dissat-
isfied (at level eight or below). If we can become better at noticing
when we are in a state of satisfaction, then we can clearly identify
when we are in the Zone of Greatness and when we are not.

Just knowing if we are in the Zone of Greatness or not helps us move
into it without even "trying." The more we get curious about what
satisfies us, the more satisfying stuff will show up. Asking at the end
of each day, "What felt satisfying today?", allows us to not only get
better at being in the Zone of Greatness, but it also clues us in on
our preferences and what we want or don't want. When we ask this
beautiful little question at the end of the day, it is a fantastic way to
Make Tomorrow Better Than Today.

Notice that there is very little emotional charge in this question. It's
unassuming, non-judgmental, and simple to answer. If you are like
me, you will have fun answering this writing prompt at the end of
each day.

Three Things That Felt Satisfying Today...

3 things that felt **satisfying** today...

1 ....

2 ....

3 ....

The Daily Momentum practice you will create later in the book will
give you the prompt to write three things that felt satisfying today

at the end of every day. You may discover experiences, foods, people, and music. Maybe even a new ice cream flavor that is satisfying as you ask yourself this every day. This simple prompt will naturally entice you to start being more adventurous and to experiment and become more curious about what feels satisfying. Satisfaction comes in 50 shades, just like fear. Sometimes, having a long, overdue, truthful conversation with someone could feel more satisfying than your favorite ice cream.

What did you put energy into today?

Top **3** things I put **energy** into today...

1. ....
2. ....
3. ....

The second question is, what did you put energy into today? You might also think of this as asking, "What did you focus on today?", or, "What did you put your attention on today?" Often, things are competing for, grabbing, or hijacking our attention. Recognizing when that has happened throughout your day can give you food for thought about how to handle things differently in the future.

The things we put energy into throughout the day aren't always in front of us. If we are worried or excited about something in the future, it can demand energy from us today. Sometimes, there's just one big thing demanding our attention, and it doesn't leave us with any bandwidth for anything else.

The Daily Momentum Process later in the book will give you the prompt to write the top three things that you put energy into at the end of every day. When we begin to quantify how we are investing our energy, it will naturally begin to upgrade both our activities and mindset. This prompt is also a great way to begin to see patterns or habits. We might notice that we write the same thing down day after day as what we are putting energy into. As I am writing this book, that is the case for me. But if it's not something we want to invest our energy in regularly, then we may be alerted to a big distraction that is hemorrhaging our ability to be great.

We can also discern if the things we are making a priority match the top things getting our energy. Are we walking our talk? Are we moving toward what we want?

These two powerful daily prompts are where the rubber meets the road. They alert us to whether or not we are honoring our word with ourselves and keeping our promises. Remember, though—no judgment, just curiosity as you reflect, debrief, and get curious about how you could upgrade at the end of every day.

daily rewind

At the beginning of our day, we may meticulously lay out every task, every appointment, and every minute of our day. And yet, even with the best-laid plans, life is full of surprises for us. And that is not a bad thing!

Creating Daily Momentum is a habit, not a drill sergeant, to shift us into greatness more of the time. Being in a Zone of Greatness means being intentional about how we spend our resources like time, energy, and money. It also means that we need to have enough of a reserve to be able to seize new opportunities as they show up and to have the space to be great. More about that in the next section.

When we are living in a state of greatness, we know what we want and we show up starting where we are. We set goals and plan our days, but not with tunnel vision. We need to give ourselves the freedom to change our plans, deliberately disrupt our reality, make upgrades, and reboot our day at any time that we want to.

In life, being just one degree off course can lead to drastically different outcomes. For example, if a pilot starts their journey in Los Angeles aiming for Hawaii but is just one degree off in their navigation, they could end up missing the island entirely, potentially landing hundreds of miles away in the vast Pacific Ocean.

Small navigational shifts and regular course-corrections are so critical that a pilot actually spends the majority of a flight actively engaged in course-correcting; it's not just a small part of the journey but a continuous process. Throughout the flight, a pilot is constantly making adjustments to account for factors like air traffic, weather conditions, and wind changes.

There is a prevalent limiting belief that haunts high achievers: that if we don't stick to the plan, goal, or schedule, then we are a flake. Most of the time, this couldn't be further from the truth. Flaky people are usually blindly oblivious to the fact that they are not sticking to things. The irony of this limiting belief is that if you are concerned about being flaky, then you are probably not flaky. Instead, you may be the opposite—sticking to things for the sake of it when it would actually be better to course-correct instead.

That being said, there will be some things that we may be avoiding, putting off, or not doing. Yep, back to the P-word again. How do we know if we are procrastinating and putting off something great? Notice how you are feeling. Take your emotional temperature and make intentional choices throughout the day. If you are on the lower end of the Emotional Thermometer, then start asking questions.

Procrastination-Busting Questions

- Why don't I want to do that right now?

- What am I afraid of?

- Would the great choice right now be not to do this project?

- When would be a great time to invest my time and energy in this project?

Because of all these navigational shifts throughout the day, the day you planned will not look like the day you lived most of the time. Debriefing how we actually spent our time at the end of the day allows us to recognize where and how we made great navigational choices—and where there is room for an upgrade. The Daily Rewind is a great tool that we can use to step back through our day. We retrace our steps and get curious about how our plans changed. It's a simple process that will take only a few minutes at the end of the day. And we will build it into your Daily Momentum practice later in this book.

You will want to do your Daily Rewind before you get too tired but not too early in the day that you may miss some of the things you are spending time on.

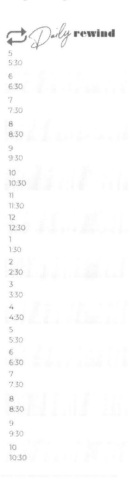

Your Daily Rewind is not just your work day; it is a rewind from the minute you open your eyes in the morning until you are ready to turn out the lights at night.

Did you oversleep?

How long did you take for lunch?

When did you start and finish your work day?

Write down everything you did in your Daily Rewind. Put as much detail as possible. The more detail, the more opportunities you will uncover to make tomorrow better than today.

daily do-overs

Within an hour of arriving at the hospital, the doctor asked me, "Are you sure you don't want a c-section?"

"No c-section," I replied. The truth was, I wasn't sure about anything; I was afraid. I had watched way too many documentaries of women going through their pregnancies and being rushed into surgery. I was afraid of someone cutting into my stomach and pulling out my baby. So afraid that I continued to refuse in the ninth hour and the nineteenth hour—until in the twenty-ninth hour, when the doctor told me, "Your baby is in danger. Are you sure you don't want a c-section?" Even though I was still scared out of my mind, I said YES! I changed my mind. If I could have had a do-over, I would have agreed the first time I was asked, not the last.

Do-overs don't imply that we did anything wrong the first time around; they are simply a way of imagining future upgrades so that we have more choices available to us in the future.

Three Daily Do-Overs

The final part of your Daily Momentum practice each day will be to answer the Do-Over Question. Now that you know how to review your day thoroughly using the debrief questions and the Daily Rewind, you are in the perfect position to go on an upgrade hunt and get curious. If you could have a do-over of the day, what you would choose to do differently?

I always find at least one thing. I don't care how perfectly the day went. Do-overs don't have to be massive changes or problems; your Daily Do-Over may simply be that you would have ordered two scoops of ice cream instead of one. Do-overs accelerate our personal and professional development and growth.

When we identify Daily Do-Overs, we open up more choices for the future to be even greater. When we ask, "What could I have done differently?", we're not judging ourselves; we're not implying that we did anything wrong—we are just getting curious and figuring out other options to choose from in the future.

From the very first time we write something down as a Daily Do-Over, that choice is now available in our future. We have literally carved out new neural pathways to store it as a viable choice. Sometimes we may sit with something we want to do differently, chewing on it for a little while like a puzzle, figuring out what the do-over would be. Don't give up. Really think it through. There are most likely many more choices available to you than you realize. It is common practice for a surgeon to mentally rehearse different procedures so that when they are under pressure in the operating room, they are ready for anything. Like a surgeon, you can mentally rehearse different ways of upgrading your days by contemplating your Daily Do-Overs at the end of each day.

My daughter and I ran out of gas on the way to the Grand Canyon once. I bet you can guess what my Daily Do-Over was that day—but it wasn't just to have put gas in the car; I rewound the day in my mind until I figured out exactly when I would have put gas in the car, which happened to be the day before. I even figured out which gas station I would have used. I want you to be that thoughtful and specific with your do-overs too.

Sometimes we might find ourselves writing down the same do-over again and again and again. There is no shame in that. We are warming ourselves up, getting ourselves ready, and pre-paving different choices for the future. That can take time.

A Daily Do-Over is not a to-do list; we are not committing to or requiring ourselves to do things differently. If you catch yourself in that mode, lovingly remind yourself that this is your old way of operating, of pushing yourself to try to change. In our Zone of Greatness, all we need to do is notice, and Zero Gravity activates upgrades, shifts, and changes so that they happen at the perfect time.

Sometimes, I find myself feeling inspired to do the Daily Do-Over right after I write it down. I might write down a do-over to tell someone I love them, and I may decide to shoot off a quick "I love you" text right then and there. As long as it feels like you are operating in your Zone of Greatness from the higher end of the Emotional Thermometer, go for it. But never push, require, or commit to taking action on any of your do-overs; otherwise, they will just become more to-dos!

Wanting to do something over doesn't mean that there was anything wrong with today. Approach this exercise knowing you did the best you could with all the variables of the day. It was already good; you are just fine-tuning it to become greater.

upgrade yourself

When I hear the word "upgrade," my thoughts immediately go to the experience of air travel and the allure of upgrading to first class. This kind of upgrade has a sense of opulence, luxury, and indulgence. It's about savoring a taste of the high life. Upgrades like flying first class often find their way onto our bucket lists. They become experiences we aspire to, at least once in our lifetime; to bask in that extraordinary feeling of comfort and privilege.

We might also see an upgrade as an indication that we have arrived, that we have achieved a goal, met a milestone, or shifted into a different lifestyle. What is funny to me is that an upgrade appears to be a big step but it's often actually quite a small change. When we upgrade to first class on an airplane, one of the main differences is a few more inches of legroom. Yes, we might also get slightly better food and better service, but primarily what we're upgrading to is just a little more space.

As we explore changes and upgrades using the tools in this section of the book, notice how space—whether time-space or physical space—is often a key motivator of change. When we have just a little more time-space, maybe an extra ten or fifteen minutes, then we can more easily shift out of rushing and pushing and into greatness. Financial space, a little more money, often allows us to feel like we have the ability and freedom to purchase whatever we want. Having more space in many ways elevates us to a new level in our lives. Primarily though, almost all upgrades satiate one of our number one desires: a desire for freedom.

Each of the approaches to change we have explored are different perspectives on change. Rebooting instead of being seen as a dead end or obstacle becomes an opportunity to start over. Pulling out the plug and putting it back in again may feel like disconnection. But if we shift perspective and see that it's a process to restart and begin again, we may feel more freedom and less like a victim of circumstances. Disrupting our reality regularly can be reframed as a choice, a way to become more intentional, get out of a rut, and discover new preferences and possibilities.

When we upgrade, we are choosing to raise the bar, lift ourselves to higher standards, and reset our default way of being. We have an internal set point or standard for everything in our lives, from the amount of money we feel comfortable having in the bank to the amount of stress we can handle. These standards then act as our default set point, like a thermostat for our heating, keeping us within strict boundaries that we have consciously or unconsciously defined.

Our defaults may be created from our experiences in life so far, our upbringing, and the environments we operate in.

When we dip below our set points, we may feel lost, overwhelmed, or even afraid. We will do anything we can to avoid these feelings of uncomfortableness. When we upgrade, we change our set point or default setting and make it the new normal. These upgrades ripple like little earthquakes of pleasure impacting all areas of our lives.

Upgrading Your Defaults

If you have ever used willpower alone to create change in your life, you know how hard that approach can be. Willpower requires vigilance. If you let your guard down for a moment, a piece of chocolate cake can easily find its way into your mouth. It has been proven that willpower diminishes throughout the day and eventually runs out. This is why it's often easier for people to eat healthily or go to the gym in the morning and harder in the evening.

And what happens when willpower runs out? We go back to our default settings, just like many electronic devices that revert to their factory settings when their battery is replaced. It is exponentially easier to create transformation, change, attain goals, and be in our greatness if instead of focusing on willpower we simply upgrade our default settings. So, why not make a new, better normal that reflects you living in greatness?

When we are exhausted and burned out, it's just easier to go back to our default settings. If we have been having a very productive day and been focused in our Zone of Greatness and then decide to push ourselves to the finish line, suddenly our project is not as much fun as it was before. Now we just want to get it done. When we push, we sacrifice our joy now for perceived joy later.

Even if we have been making really great food choices all week, when we are exhausted and hungry, we will operate from our default—because when we run out of willpower and grab something to eat, we will most likely go for whatever our default is.

Here is the exciting point: if we have already chosen to deliberately upgrade our default, perhaps in one of our Daily Do-Overs a few weeks ago, then our go-to choices for food have been pre-paved for us, even when we are tired and burned out. We may realize we have a healthy smoothie in the fridge instead of our old go-to of cheese and crackers or a brownie.

Upgrading is not only about flying first class and having bucket-list luxurious peak moments occasionally; it's about upgrading your default settings so that you can live most of your life as an upgrade, not a roller coaster ride. Instead of living life with moments where you are flying high in between plummeting down again, why not raise the bar to a new normal?

How do we recognize and identify our default set points? Begin to notice what your go-tos are when you are at the lower end of the Emotional Thermometer. Look at what you tend to do when you are out of willpower, tired, hungry, uninspired, and unmotivated. And then get curious about what you could do differently, what the do-over might be, and create new neural pathways little by little. Before you know it, your default setting will be first class and you will be imagining a private jet. Don't laugh—remember Giselle who was afraid of public speaking earlier in the book? That's exactly what she did!

make tomorrow better than today cheat sheet

Do you really want a problem-free life? What does that even mean? Instead, perhaps seek to find better problems. When we upgrade the problems in our lives, we make conscious choices to uncover new, better problems to solve. You can use any of the tools we have learned in this section of the book focused on the Greatness Habit Three: Make Tomorrow Better Than Today, to create change by rebooting, upgrading, or deliberately disrupting your reality anytime you like.

Greatness happens when we set goals that are aligned with our desires and dreams and refuse to let life make our choices for us. It happens when we ask questions. Greatness is always there to guide us when we choose to listen. Greatness can happen when we realize that the road forward may not be a smooth ride and we are willing to take it anyway.

We need problems to move us so that we can invite the solutions to just show up for us by using questions. Greatness gives us the strength to move past the problem into solution-thinking so that we can get to the pool on a cold November morning to swim laps, drive to the yoga studio when we just want to stay in our PJs, and rehearse our presentation even though our fear of public speaking feels paralyzing.

The next time you feel burned out or can't seem to stick to things, you know when you are in the vicinity of that mythical beast: procrastination. Do a debrief by simply asking, "If I could do things differently, what could I do?" to give yourself an upgrade.

If we are hungry for our goals, we can step up and stand out from the rest of the people in the race. We can choose better problems to solve and embrace our greatness. We can give ourselves permission to experiment with new ways of being again and again, feeling our way forward.

Download the cheat sheet for Greatness Habit Three: Make Tomorrow Better Than Today as well as the Daily Debrief Worksheet at www.dailymomentumhub.com

We are all constantly evolving. It is 100% okay to change your mind. You're not a flake; change equals growth. If you want to grow—which we all do, as it's the point of life—then something has to change. We have to choose differently. We have to choose to make tomorrow better than today.

HABIT FOUR

create space to be great

"Got to walk out of here, I can't take any more. Gonna stand on that bridge, keep my eyes down below. Whatever may come and whatever may go, that river's flowing, that river's flowing."

—Peter Gabriel

nothing

"Cause nothing compares. Nothing compares to you."

—Sinéad O'Connor

I first met Mary "Mu" at a South Pasadena Chamber business mixer. A new local children's dentist had opened and was selected as the venue that month. Fifty eager business owners showed up, and we were all squished in between dentist chairs, hygienist tools, and drills, exchanging business cards with quick, clumsy conversations.

I began making the rounds, and out of the corner of my eye, I saw a beautiful woman striding around the perimeter of the room with a baby swaddled across her chest. Over the next sixty minutes, as I mixed and mingled, her energy kept tugging on me. I chatted with insurance salesmen, local dignitaries, and real estate agents until finally, I made my way through the crowd and my path was clear to talk to this woman who had so captivated my attention.

"Hello, my name is Marianne," I introduced myself, and so our relationship began. My most devoted student, my greatest teacher, and a loyal and loving friend had entered my life.

Mu had just opened her acupuncture practice and showed up at every South Pasadena Chamber event with her white coat on. I invited her to be part of my new women in business group. She told me with love and coolness, "I say no to everything at first." Then she smiled and said, "And maybe later I will say yes. So, don't stop asking."

So, I didn't. After six months, Mu joined our women in business group, and as she left the first meeting, I could feel that she had found her community; but more importantly, we were lucky to have her be a part of it.

Mu showed up to our meetings religiously over the next nine years. She may say "no" to things at first; however, when she did say "yes," it was a strong, solid, powerful YES! It's a YES with her whole being. It is a yes that invites you into her life and brings with it a level of dedication, commitment, and loyalty that I have experienced only a few times in my life. This is why it is important for her to say "no" first. She needs to honor the space to be great because it is sacred. This was the first lesson of many that Mu taught me.

Mu was the only person who referred to me simply as "Coach." There was a reverence, humor, and respect in her using that term. She always had a cheeky twinkle in her eye as she said, "Hello, Coach," "Yes, Coach," or, "Thank you, Coach."

When I asked Mu about her name, she gave me that mischievous smile again and let me know it meant "nothingness" or "nonexistence." She continued to share that, in the context of Zen Buddhism, "Mu" is used as a way of answering a question beyond yes or no to find an answer that lies beyond binary thinking. Mu is a way of telling someone to think outside of the box or look at a problem differently. Suddenly, she made so much more sense to me.

Mu loved systems and tools and immediately embraced the lessons I introduced to the ladies during our monthly meetings. After every meeting, usually in a text or email, she expressed her appreciation for what we had learned that day, for the space I had created, and for the way I had shown up.

She challenged me too. Mu was the first to let me know if a tool didn't quite work or if something was missing. And if she was missing a piece of the puzzle, she would keep letting me know about it, nudging me until I listened and brought her the missing piece.

That is exactly what happened with WordPress. Mu wanted to build a website using WordPress, a software platform for building websites. I had used different software for building my first website but was also interested in moving it to WordPress, but I kept getting stuck with how to do it. But there was this little bug in my ear. Mu kept saying, "You should teach a WordPress class." I waved it away at first, but eventually, I sat down and finally figured out WordPress and built my first website in it.

Now that I was an expert (after building one website) I was ready. "Okay, Mu, I am going to teach the class," I told her. And right away, she signed up for my new class, "Website in a Day." And what a day it was. I gathered all the ladies together with their computers and we began the exhausting adventure. There were a few loose ends that we tied up in the second part of the class, but for the most part, all the ladies left with a website in a day. I was exhausted. My head hurt but not as much as my thighs did from bobbing up and down helping each lady at her computer for eight hours straight.

This is how Mu shaped the Women's Business Momentum Center over the nine years she was a part of it. She asked for what she needed relentlessly until she understood it and then would express the most sincere, loving, and beautiful words of gratitude.

She wanted upgrades to the planner I created for the group, so I added them. I began offering retreats, but Mu wanted more of them. And, of course, she had immense gratitude and joy to share with me once she fondly received all of her requests.

Those retreats created some of the most precious memories of my life. Women came together, bunking together, cooking and eating together. As they laughed, splashed in the pool, sobbed, and celebrated, they shared the experience of creating, growing, and sometimes letting go of a business.

Mu would always share a room with Joanna or "Lady Vargas" as she liked to call her. One time they were both sick, sniffling and sleeping through most of the retreat. Even so, you would hear Joanna's loud, roaring laughter echoing through the house as she nurtured her soul with funny videos; it somehow beautifully complemented Mu's quieter personality.

Mu lost her battle with cancer in the summer of 2019. I am now grateful to have the room that Mu and Joanna shared as my home office and mediation space. I have adorned the walls with pictures of all the ladies. It feels so right to have Mu with me there as I work, reminding me how powerful it can be to say no first then maybe later a yes, to ask for what you want and to express heartfelt gratitude often. I learned to challenge myself to find an answer beyond yes and no and how deeply precious nothing can be.

under-promise

When we over-extend ourselves by saying "yes" to more things than we can physically and mentally handle, we over-promise and under-deliver. We may under-deliver on a project for ourselves or someone else, and when we do, we are left feeling disappointed. This feeling of disappointment arises because the reality we are now facing does not match how we imagined it would be. We did not get what we expected. Anytime we feel disappointed in ourselves, we make a withdrawal from our emotional bank account. We deflate our sense of hope and excitement and move further down the Emotional Thermometer and away from our Zone of Greatness.

On the other hand, when we under-promise and over-deliver, we feel a sense of accomplishment and satisfaction, which moves us up the Emotional Thermometer and increases our sense of greatness and our productivity. It is so much easier to stay in the magical Zone of Greatness if we are operating emotionally from the upper section of the Emotional Thermometer. We want to do whatever we can to better manage our expectations and avoid making withdrawals from our emotional bank account.

Often, if projects, goals, or tasks are not clearly defined, they don't get done. Just setting a clear expectation of the basics of what we are going to do, how long it will take, and even why we are doing it can easily help us shift from over-promising to under-promising and, in doing so, make a substantial deposit rather than withdrawing from our emotional bank account.

As we move into the Greatness Habit Four: Create the Space to Be Great, I will share tools, strategies, and insights to help you under-promise and over-deliver. The beauty of this premise is that it is a mindset we can create before we start taking action. It gives us a way of showing up in greatness before we start our day, to set the tone and pre-pave the best experience possible.

Now, we all know that everything won't go exactly as planned; we talked about that in the previous section of the book when we explored the Daily Rewind. It doesn't matter; it is still a game changer to plan our day. When we mentally rehearse the day and get crystal clear on our expectations, we pave the way for greatness.

One of the simplest ways to under-promise and over-deliver each day is by shifting the way we organize our time. As we plan our day and start creating that good-old to-do list, get into the habit of defining how much time a task will take. Write it down next to the task. Then, after you write down how long you think it will take, triple it.

This is a strategy I have used with clients for decades to help them begin to shift from over-promising to under-promising and over-delivering. I call it "the 3 X Rule."

From my experience of working with contractors, they seem to have a habit of over-promising and under-delivering. It's not because they want the work to take longer but because they want to please the client and keep them happy. Often, we get into a habit of over-promising because we want to keep everyone happy, and so we tell them what they want to hear. That is not necessarily the exact truth. If we catch ourselves slipping into a habit of under-delivering, then we are probably over-promising. This is not just with other people but with ourselves too. Over-promising is a way to keep the itty-bitty-shitty committee in our heads quiet for a while. But it doesn't last.

If I hire a contractor to work on my home, what I've learned over the years is that when the contractor tells me how long something's going to take, most of the time, it takes about three times as long—probably because they want to please me. They are afraid that if they tell me something I don't want to hear, I will hire someone else. Over-promising may seem like a way to keep people happy or to get them to leave us alone and quit bugging us, but it comes at a high cost.

Things happen that are outside of our control, and it is NORMAL for things to take longer than we expect. And yes, there are some amazing contractors out there who are over-delivering and meeting deadlines, but the natural human tendency is to underestimate, not overestimate, time.

It's not like anyone is trying to be deceptive; we want to please people, including ourselves, by telling the story everyone wants to hear. We run into unanticipated snags, get distracted, life shows up, and delays happen. But, if we build in three times the amount of time we need, then the worst thing that can happen is we over-deliver, finish sooner, and end up with some time to spare. We create space to be great.

If we get into the habit of 3 X our day and our projects, we gradually get better at estimating how long things will take. Then eventually, we may move to 2 X or even be able to exactly gauge how long something will take, with time to spare.

Until then, triple the amount of time you think something will take, especially with new tasks, to-dos, or projects. That way, you can prevent withdrawals from your emotional bank account and stay in momentum.

Once you start to see how much space, freedom, and focus under-promising and over-delivering creates, you will begin to do it with everything, and that's when things will really get fun.

prime time

We have approximately four to four and a half hours of prime working time each day. Prime Time refers to the period when an individual's mental focus, energy, and productivity are at their highest, enabling them to perform tasks more efficiently and effectively. This window varies from person to person but is typically when we are most alert and capable of producing our greatest work. Prime Time creates the space where we can be great!

A study highlighted by the job website Zippia reveals that the average employee is productive for about 4.8 hours per day, with office employees clocking in even less at around 2 hours and 53 minutes of effective work time daily. This is complemented by another study, also reported by Zippia, which found that in an 8-hour workday, the average worker is actively engaged in work for only about 4 hours and 12 minutes.

These studies challenge our conventional views on workplace efficiency and productivity. They suggest that instead of stretching our work across a standard eight-hour period, focusing on maximizing these prime four to four and a half hours could be more beneficial.

What if you were to shift toward a more flexible, results-oriented work model, where the emphasis is on productive output rather than time spent? Adapting our work schedules to align with our natural productivity peaks could lead not only to more efficiency but also more satisfying work experiences. If we tap into the times when we are most focused and creative, we get more done! The Daily Momentum process will help you build your actions around your Prime Time each day.

Let's take a deeper look at Prime Time

Healthline magazine published an article on sleep chronotypes that may help you figure out when your Prime Time is each day.

The *Healthline* article references a study by Eva Cohen, a certified sleep science coach who uses four animals as chronotypes, each with a different preferred window for their four and a half hours of Prime Time each day.

The Lion

According to *Healthline*, "Lion chronotypes like to rise early in the morning. They may easily wake up before dawn and are at their best up until noon. Typically, lion types wind down in the evening and end up falling asleep by 9 pm or 10 pm." Prime Time for a lion chronotype is from 8 am to noon.

The Bear

Healthline reports that, "Most people fall under the category of a bear chronotype. This means their sleep and wake cycle goes according to the sun." Cohen says bear chronotypes wake easily and typically fall asleep with no problem. Productivity seems best before 1 pm, and they're prone to the "post-lunch" dip between 2 pm and 4 pm. The Bear chronotype Prime Time to focus is usually from 9 am to 1 pm.

The Wolf

This chronotype often has trouble waking up in the morning. In fact, Cohen says, "Wolf chronotypes feel more energetic when they wake up at noon, especially since their peak productivity starts at noon and ends about 4 hours later." Wolf types also get another boost around 6 pm and find they can get a lot done while everyone else is done for the day. Wolves don't like going to bed much before midnight, which sounds a lot like my husband. The wolf's window of Prime Time focus is from noon to 2 pm or 4 pm and then again another boost around 6 pm.

The Dolphin

"If you have trouble following any sleep schedule, then you may be a dolphin," reports *Healthline*. "They often don't get enough sleep due to their sensitivity to different disturbing factors like noise and light," says Cohen." The good news? Dolphins have a peak productivity window of Prime Time from 10 am to 2 pm, which is a great time to get things done.

Realizing that your prime working time spans approximately four to four and a half hours each day opens up a world of possibilities. We do great work when our mental focus and productivity are at their peak. The concept of Prime Time can transform how we work. This is not about working longer but instead about leveraging those Prime Time hours for maximum productivity, whatever you are doing. Embracing this approach could free up significant time, giving you more space to be great every day.

Experiment with identifying your Prime Time. Whether you're a morning lion or a nocturnal wolf, aligning your daily schedule to your natural productivity rhythm can be a game changer.

pre-pave

Time is a powerful resource that we can choose to leverage or we can allow to become a ball and chain around our neck. The next tools we will learn, Power Hours and Time Blocking, will help us set up our day so that we spend more time in our Zone of Greatness.

Time is a form of currency. As we work toward an important goal, we may feel like we need more money. Money can often feel like a major roadblock. We might feel like we could get so much more done if we had more money—whether it's to get new inventory, hire a maid, pay for coaching and training, or build a new website. But in actuality, our number one currency is time, not money. When we start to look at time as our number one asset, we can dramatically shift how we spend it. We could have all the money in the world, but without time, it's useless.

Instead of just looking at how to generate more money, what if you also put energy into becoming more efficient with how you spend your time? Time Blocking and Power Hours are an easy way to quickly upgrade your relationship with time and how you choose to spend your most valuable asset.

We can make small changes to create big upgrades in how we spend our time. I encourage you to create space at the beginning of every day to pause and look at your schedule, then intentionally decide what it is you're going to do, when you are going to do it, and what your Daily One Thing is. In the upcoming Daily Momentum section of the book, I will help you put all of the tools you need into your Daily Momentum practice and set up your morning and evening routines.

The energy we invest in planning and preparing is equally, if not more, important than the energy we put into doing "stuff." We can create much more flow and ease if we mentally prepare before we jump into action. When we stop and think more intentionally about how we spend our time, we are "pre-paving."

Pre-paving is the concept of mentally preparing and setting positive intentions about how you want an upcoming situation or event to unfold. The author Abraham Hicks describes it as the power of our thoughts in shaping our experiences. By focusing on positive outcomes in advance, we can influence the trajectory of our lives. As Hicks puts it, "Pre-paving is deliberately thinking thoughts that feel good with the intention of laying the groundwork for that which you want to be, do, or have to come more easily." When we pre-pave our day before we dive into action, we create the space to be great and maximize our time so that we can own our day.

It can sometimes feel tempting to skip the step of pre-paving because we want to just get into action. You might feel the impulse to rush and create a quick list instead of intentionally contemplating how you are going to invest your time each day. Checking things off a list feeds into our human desire to finish things. It is a good way of operating, but not a great one. We get an endorphin rush when we check things off our list. Investing time to stop, pause, and pre-pave your day and create an intentional plan may even feel like a waste of time at first, but if we prioritize just checking items off the list over making a great list to begin with, we can fall prey to "fake work."

Fake work is busywork that feels productive but lacks real value and doesn't actually move us forward toward our goals or create any real progress. In our personal lives, fake work might look like constantly organizing and reorganizing your home without getting rid of clutter or making any meaningful, lasting improvements. Professionally, fake work may look like attending networking events with no intentions of really meeting anyone or following up. Fake work may give us a shallow sense of accomplishment at the end of the day only to look around later and wonder why we are working so hard and not getting anywhere. Being more intentional with how we spend our time means looking at why we are doing what we are doing, not just how, what, and when. When we are clear on our why, we can quickly identify fake work when it shows up, avoid it, and make better use of our time. This more intentional approach also upgrades the quality of our work.

If we are working on a big project, like writing a book, we need to stop periodically and remind ourselves why we are doing it. Asking ourselves questions like who we're writing the book for (the audience) and what the purpose of the book is enables us to stay focused. Otherwise, we may lose the plot and write 500 meaningless, meandering pages that are more confusing than helpful to the reader. We can use this intentional approach for all our projects, tasks, and even how we plan our days. When we do, we notice more confidence about our projects, and our focus will dramatically improve. Suddenly, all those distractions creating so much noise quickly disappear, and procrastination loses its power.

Pre-paving is an essential part of getting stuff done. Thinking about what a project, task, or goal might look like in advance enables us to forge a clearer path forward and minimize the detours. Whether it's redecorating our home, eating healthier, or hosting a family celebration, spending just a few minutes pre-paving will create more successful outcomes that are in-line with our expectations and measurable process toward our goals.

Pre-paving is the first step in shifting our relationship with how we spend our time. When we manage our expectations better and see and believe that we can have more flow, ease, and productivity in our days, then we are primed to create change. The next step is to intentionally carve out the time to get stuff done and design your day around time blocks.

time-blocking

Who is in charge of your time? When you own the fact that you are the one in charge of your time, you are also acknowledging that you always have a choice in how you spend it. Even if you are employed in a day job, you may still be able to negotiate some of the boundaries around your time, such as how late you stay in the evening or when you take a lunch break. Reminding yourself, no matter what situation you are in, that you are the one in charge of your time is essential if you want to create the space you need to be great.

Once we acknowledge that we are the ones in charge of our schedule, we become much more comfortable placing boundaries around our time. Our time may even begin to feel like more of a valuable asset to us than it did before. Time blocking is a great tool to help us to better manage how we spend our time. It allows us to intentionally block off different parts of our schedule in advance for different activities. When every task, One Thing, or project has a time and place, it is less likely to get lost and forgotten. When we intentionally time-block our days and our weeks, we can clearly see what will fit into our schedule and what will not. This helps us prioritize better and make better choices about how we spend our precious time.

Time blocks are simply a snazzy way of describing blocks of time with a clear start and end point. Think of them as Lego blocks. Just as we can put together different-sized blocks to build a Lego house, we can also organize our day with different time blocks. We might use 25-minute time blocks, also known as the Pomodoro Technique (25 minutes of activity followed by a 5-minute break), 90-minute time blocks, or maybe 50-minute blocks. When we time-block, we are instantly being more intentional about how we are using our time and what we are doing. Any time I use the phrase "time block," feel free to interpret it as a time block of the length of your choice.

Without time blocks, our day blends into one; it's a long 500-meter ocean swim. Projects, to-dos, and even important deadlines can easily get lost and forgotten without clear time slots in place to accommodate them—especially if we are not creating a distinction between our work activities and our personal activities, which is a common danger for business owners and high-achieving professionals.

Knowing what we want to achieve and why, within the different segments of our day, helps us more easily discern what is important and what is not. With that knowledge, we can create more efficient time blocks within our day. If we also develop a habit of setting a

Daily One Thing, it can give us even clearer direction and better focus throughout the day. Our Daily One Thing helps us remember what is most important today.

How much structure do we need? Enough to create the space to be great! If we add too many time blocks and build too much structure into our day, we may feel like we have no space to catch our breath. Our creativity may be limited, and we might just feel like we are on a treadmill going nowhere. Not enough time blocks may leave us feeling lost and overwhelmed and opens the door to procrastination and distractions.

Experiment with time-blocking your schedule in advance and see how you feel on the Emotional Thermometer as you look at the day you have planned on the page. Even adding just one time block to each day may allow you to feel more confident, organized, and productive.

Time blocks give us a way of organizing our activities into different buckets. We may have time blocks for rest and renewal, exercise, eating meals, and recreation. In our professional lives, we may include time blocks for administrative activities, customer service, marketing, sales, and working IN and ON our business, if we have one.

Beware of time-blocking an entire day without building in breaks, meals, and time to rest and renew. Experiment and recognize how each day is unique and has different needs. You may feel more energized and be able to take on more time blocks one day, while another day, you may need more time for renewal built in. This is why, even if we plan our week ahead—which I recommend—we also take the time to pre-pave each day in the morning. This creates checks and balances, before we get into action, to make sure we use our resources of time and energy wisely.

Power Hours

Power Hours are highly focused 60-minute time blocks very intentionally set up for maximum productivity. Power Hours work best when placed in our Prime Time when we are at our best. Don't overdo it, though—less is more. If every time block in our day is a Power Hour then we lose the effectiveness of this tool. Just like if we fasted every day, all the benefits we could receive would be canceled out by overdoing it. Power Hours are a time of concentration and attention focused on a specific result or milestone for a project. Often, these are projects that are not urgent but are important and would make the most impact on the trajectory of your future. These types of projects need all the help they can get to not get trampled by all the urgent activities and distractions that can show up each day. You might reserve your Power Hours for moving forward on your One Thing and add one or maybe two to each day before you time-block the rest of your day.

Pre-paving our day using a combination of time blocks and Power Hours is a more productive way to schedule our activities than just using a long to-do list and winging it. Time-blocking requires us to think more intentionally about what we are going to do, how long it might take, and what other activities we want to build around it to help us be more productive. This allows us to create Winning Environments that bring more ease, flow, and confidence to our activities.

Winning Environments

A long time ago, I watched the first season of *The Biggest Loser*. The show was about a group of men and women over several weeks who were living in the same house, and it followed their weight loss journey.

To create drama, the producers of the show filled the house with candy, sweets, and potato chips. It was a house of temptation that would actually trigger most people to do the opposite of losing weight. There were doughnuts all over the countertops, candy on the dining room table, and all kinds of fried chicken, fries, and chips all around. The fridge was stuffed with food that would quickly add calories to make the contestants' weight-loss journey even harder. It was all a big tease. The producers of the show wanted the participants to have a hard time, to raise the stakes as they all fought for the title of The Biggest Loser.

Every day, we create drama for ourselves in exactly the same way. We surround ourselves with losing instead of Winning Environments. What and who you are around directly influences who you will be. Each day, we navigate through physical, social, and economic environments. As we do, our environment rubs off on us, just like in *The Biggest Loser*.

And guess what? The environment almost always wins! So, why not put yourself on the winning team and deliberately design Winning Environments.

> "You are the average of the five people you spend the most time with."
>
> —Jim Rohn

If *The Biggest Loser* producers had wanted to create a Winning Environment for weight loss, the house would have looked very different. There would have been fresh produce all over the countertops and beautiful pitchers of water with cucumber, mint, and lemon. The house would be full of healthy food, positive statements, and pictures of people eating healthily. There would have been delicious healthy recipes with images that would make you drool. And in that environment, there would be very little drama and conflict.

The producers of *The Biggest Loser* wanted to set the contestants up to fail. The contestants were pushed to work out hard each day and were worn down and tired. At the end of the day, when they ran out of willpower, the tempting environment was there waiting to move them away from the finish line, not toward it.

If our environment is not supporting us and helping us easily make the choices we want, it is working against us, not for us. We rarely find ourselves in a neutral environment. If you look around, you will quickly see your environments are either winning ones or losing ones.

The irony is that we create many of our environments ourselves. We shop, we fill our cupboards, we place the cookbooks on the shelf, and we decide what to put in the fridge. I'm sure, like me, you have had a moment where you've been hungry, you open the fridge, and the only thing there is carbs or candy. You are starving, and there are no healthy options in sight. If it's been a long day and you are tired or it's late and you have no willpower left, of course you make the unhealthy choice. Then your itty-bitty-shitty-committee starts screaming at you and you begin to slide down the Emotional Thermometer. Who created this drama? Yep, it was all you. The good news is, now that you know, you can intentionally design your day around Winning Environments instead.

Small changes in your environment make a big impact. When you organize your client files, update your bank account, or get rid of clothes in your closet, not only are you upgrading your environment to a winning one, but you are also invigorating yourself with the energy of change. Simple things like opening up your closet and being able to quickly grab the clothes that make you feel good when you wear them changes how you show up in the world.

If you place pampering things in the bathroom—perhaps gifts that were bought for you that had been hidden away—now when you shower, you feel special, and your senses are brought to life. As you begin to play with Winning Environments, you are also creating a domino effect of changes that will ripple through all the areas of your life.

Now that you can see how pivotal your environments are in creating changes in your actions, behavior, and emotions, you can begin to design your environments to create more productivity in your time blocks and activities each day. You can design your environments to work for you instead of against you.

The physical and social environment that we are working in will have a direct impact on how successful we are in each of our time blocks and Power Hours. The easiest way to create change is to notice something that is not working and then use a question like, "What else is possible?" to help you begin to design a Winning Environment instead.

If we need the internet to work on a project during a time block and we happen to be working in a place with patchy internet, we're putting ourselves in a losing environment. Instead, we can shuffle our time blocks around so that maybe we are working on brainstorming a new book or memorizing a new presentation while in a location without internet. Then we turn our losing environment into a winning one and having no internet becomes a benefit.

Choose to put yourself into Winning Environments for your activities whenever you can. Don't settle for less than optimum; if you do, you end up wasting time and moving slower on your projects. Walking, sitting in an office, being outside, and even what you are wearing can dictate whether you are in a losing or a Winning Environment. The powerful combo of time blocking, Power Hours, and Winning Environments can propel you into Zero Gravity and have a massive impact on how productive you are each day.

What Role Are You Playing Next?

We wear so many different hats throughout the day. As you step into a time block, consider asking yourself, "What role am I playing next?" Maybe even come up with fun, creative job titles for your role in each time block. Instead of telling yourself you are sitting down to write, you can choose to be "*The New York Times'* Best-Selling Author" sitting down to finish Chapter 12. At different times throughout each day, you may be the secretary, the technician, the coach, or the massage therapist for a coworker. You may be the accountant, the social media expert, or the best-selling author. When your head is in the right space for the role you are playing, you can then better determine how to design the Winning Environment for each time block. Defining which role we are playing as we step into a time block will not only help us focus, but it can also spark our imagination and tame our expectations. More about that in the next chapter.

tame expectations

What do you expect to get done during your time blocks? At first, you may just be guessing, but that's okay—you are going to get better at managing your expectations the more you challenge yourself to be upfront about them. Start by asking yourself, "What do I expect to accomplish by the end of this time block?" Take a moment to write this down before you begin the time block. Set your expectations as well as your intentions.

When I first began being honest with myself about my expectations, it was comical. I began by writing down what I thought I was going to achieve in a week. At the time, I was really into lists and didn't know about mind mapping. I got all fired up making a big, long list of what I expected to get done by the end of the week.

After just a few weeks of doing this, it became very clear that my expectations were completely out of touch with my reality. The list I was writing for the week was honestly more like a month or even a year's worth of activities, to-dos, and projects. It felt really good to write it all down; it got me motivated, and then I would excitedly get into action. But pretty quickly, as I began to fall short of my very long list, it became disheartening. I would run out of steam as I made massive withdrawals from my emotional bank account.

To begin with, the process of writing my lists of expectations down felt like a roller coaster. But I continued to commit to writing them down at the beginning of every day, and after just a few days, my list began to get smaller. I started to notice that at the end of each day, what I had expected to get done had perhaps been a little ambitious. I had over-promised. When this happened day after day, as I was making the list at the beginning of the day, I was able to recognize that I was over-promising. Then I began to learn how to under-promise and take things off the list before the day began.

This way, at the end of the day, I found myself feeling more satisfied and getting a higher percentage of my now shorter list accomplished. Life felt less like a roller coaster and more like a fun, if slightly bumpy, road. I had learned through my own experience to tame my expectations and under-promise and over-deliver. And it felt fantastic, so of course I wanted to continue.

We can stretch ourselves to do a little bit more. But there's a big difference between expecting to finish creating our website in the next sixty minutes and setting an expectation that we are going to complete one page of our website in the same amount of time. Our expectations dramatically affect how we feel regardless of whether or not we write them down. We all have expectations about everything! Expectations live in our heads. What's great is that it's really quite simple to manage and re-calibrate your expectations. All you have to do is let them out of your head and onto the page. This simple step is magical! As you get into the habit of pre-paving your day, you will learn to laugh at yourself when you see you are over-promising. Challenge yourself to be clearer and more specific, and when you do, you will create the space to be great each day.

So many projects, goals, or tasks we take on or assign ourselves are not clearly defined. Just setting a clear expectation of the basics—what we are going to do, how long it will take, and how far we expect to get in the next time block—is all it takes to shift us from over-promising to under-promising. Then we can make a substantial deposit in our emotional bank account instead of a withdrawal.

Time-blocking allows us to create boundaries around our time and sharpen our focus for concentrated chunks of time. And don't forget about the 3 X rule. As you get clear on your expectations around your daily schedule, play with three times the amount of time you think you need.

a better list

As we create the space to be great, I have covered some powerful tools and strategies to help you plan your day, but what about the good-old to-do list? In this chapter, we are going to give your to-do list an upgrade so that it creates the space for you to be great.

Our brains are far more complex and intricate than a simple list. Imagine your brain as an ecosystem full of diverse connections rather than a straight line of orderly items. When we rely solely on lists for organizing thoughts or tasks, we might just be capturing the "'squirrels"—the immediate, scattered thoughts that are jumping around in our minds at the moment, not necessarily the most important stuff. Sure, lists are fantastic for grocery shopping and ensuring my husband remembers the kombucha, but they don't always align with the brain's natural way of processing information.

This is where the power of mind mapping comes into play. Mind mapping speaks to our brain in its native language—a language of connections, links, and associations. It's like translating our thoughts into a format that our brain understands and appreciates. By using mind mapping as a brainstorming tool before we create lists, we can tap into the deeper, more significant thoughts and ideas dwelling in the various corners of our minds. Mind mapping is a creative problem-solving technique that aligns with how our brain naturally functions, ensuring that what ends up on our lists truly reflects our priorities and not just the fleeting thoughts of the moment. Mind mapping has become an indispensable tool for me, a growth tool that I can't imagine living without. It's the bridge between the brain's intricate pathways and a Better List.

EXERCISE | A BETTER LIST

Step 1 | Mind Map

Start with a plain sheet of paper. Draw a small circle in the middle, roughly the size of a large coin. This central circle in any mind map is our main idea or theme.

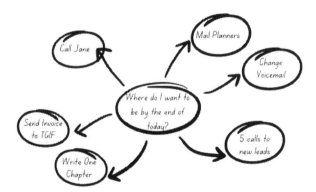

If you want to mind map as part of your daily planning, then the central theme would be a question like, "Where do I want to be by the end of today?" Next, draw lines out from this circle, connecting them to other words in smaller circles that relate to the question. Instead of just listing out all the things you want to accomplish, change, create, eliminate, or just get done today, place each item in its own circle on the page.

This simple method helps you visually organize your thoughts, helping you create a more comprehensive and focused to-do list. In the mind mapping stage of your daily planning, it's a free-for-all. You are brainstorming, so don't limit yourself by editing what you write down—anything is welcome on the page. If it is in your head right now, get it down on the page. If it's a thought, then it's most likely an expectation, and if you don't acknowledge it in this step, it could hijack your day.

Step 2 | Cherry Pick

Next, look at the mind map and identify the things you might like to include on your Daily To-Do List today. If you like, you can number them in no particular order, so they stand out on the mind map; maybe add a star to them or highlight them.

Then count them. I love playing games, and the game today could be five items or less! Keep eliminating and counting until you have five items, and then write them in any order on your Daily To-Do List in pencil. We are not done yet! The number doesn't matter, so you can figure out the sweet spot for you. Maybe it's three items or it could be ten. It just needs to be a little or even a lot less than the total of items you have written on your mind map.

Now you have used mind mapping to create a list, but is it the best list? I'm going to ask you some questions to help you play with it to upgrade it to a Better List.

Step 3 | Be Realistic

First, I want you to go down all the items on the list and next to each one write how long you think it will take you to complete it. If any of the to-dos will take you longer than thirty minutes, then it's probably not a to-do; it is a project.

Projects are made up of a series of actions. To-dos are individual tasks or very small projects that usually take less than thirty minutes to complete. Whew! Can you take that in? Did I just completely change the meaning of a to-do list for you? I hope so.

If you have items on your list that are actually projects, you can approach them one of three ways. The first way is to break the project into to-dos instead of having them as one item on the Daily To-Do List. Maybe it needs to be two or three.

Option two is to think about the project and where you would like to be with it by the end of the day. This could mean finishing a smaller chunk that could then be one or more to-dos instead of expecting to finish the entire project today.

The final option is to remove the project from the list completely and schedule it for another time in the future or add it to a back-burner list. This will probably cause some reshuffling on your list, so use a pencil and eraser.

A great question to ask yourself as you are looking at your list is, "Will this list fit in the time I have today?" Add up how long each item will take you to do and then look at your daily schedule. Will the list you have in front of you fit into today? What might you have to shift or change to make this list fit better into your day? One of the ways to measure your greatness is how much spaciousness you feel each day. Time space or padding around appointments on your schedule gives you the space to breathe and be creative. This creates the space for great ideas and the time to show up fully to execute them so that you can show up in your Zone of Greatness each day.

Step 4 | Pre-Pave

Once you have your Daily To-Do List, here are some more questions to help you build an even Better List.

Look at the items on your list. Do you feel a sense of excitement or dread? If there is something on your list that you don't want to do or that feels scary, ask yourself, "How can I upgrade this item?"

If you need to complete a project for someone else that you already committed to but really aren't excited about doing, how can you shift it? Can you think of a fun place to do it rather than at your desk? Or could you find someone to do it with you or for you?

Writing down "co-create new client proposal with Marcie" instead of "work with Marcie on client proposal" may be all it takes. Sometimes all you need is to change a word and suddenly a to-do item feels so much more fun.

Finally, look over the list and imagine, "What will this create?" How will doing these things change your life? What will be different once you have done them? If what you see in your imagination is NOT moving you forward toward what you truly want, then change the list until it is moving you toward a future that you do want. Your Daily to-do list doesn't have to completely transform your life in one day, but it should support you in taking some small steps toward the future you want.

You might be wondering about all the things that didn't make the cut. What about the items NOT on your Better List? In the next chapter, we will come back to an idea I introduced earlier in the book: our Daily NOT-To-Do List.

daily not-to-do list

Saying "no" is the new yes. Let's turn our to-do lists upside down and explore a new reality where skipping a task is a reason to do a victory dance.

In a recent Weekly Momentum, I introduced a new, innovative idea to my members: the NOT-To-Do List. I shared a little about this idea at the beginning of the book. The NOT-To-Do List isn't just a trendy idea; it can complement or even perhaps replace our traditional to-do lists. As we pre-pave our day and think about what we want to do, what if we also made a list of what to avoid or eliminate?

The method of creating our NOT-To-Do List is simple. Divide a list into two columns: one column for "to-do" and one for "not-to-do" items, with the latter including tasks that take away from our goals or are unproductive. As we do, we may very well realize where to find even more valuable space to be great.

When we add something to our NOT-To-Do List, it's okay to do so without feeling the need to explain or justify why. Our NOT-To-Do List is an unapologetic way for us to choose to focus on what's most important to us today.

Moving tasks from our to-do list to our NOT-To-Do List can free up space for creativity and more meaningful work. We are making intentional choices so that we can concentrate on what truly matters to us. This steers us away from just being busy so that we can be more effective, creative, and great in our actions every day.

Creating a NOT-To-Do List involves a thoughtful assessment of our current tasks. It's not just a matter of picking up the scraps after we mind map and go through the steps in the last chapter to create a Better List. If we want to really embrace the concept of a NOT-To-Do List, then we need to invest the time to identify which activities, as well as tasks, can be postponed or eliminated today.

How much time are you wasting each day?

According to a study run by Adam Grant, a leading organizational psychologist at Wharton University of Pennsylvania, we check email seventy-four times a day on average. What if your Not-To-Do List helped you create boundaries around this and included the instruction NOT to check email in your Prime Time today? Think about what you could NOT do that would add more time, energy, and space to your day today. Remember, it's not forever; these items are just being added to today's NOT-To-Do List.

Here are some more NOT-To-Do List ideas:

- How about not saying "yes" to scheduling anything new for the day?

- Would today be better if you said "no" to snacking—or, dare I say, chocolate?

- Maybe you could not check social media today?

- My awesome Aunty Barbara says "no" to a glass of wine on Mondays, Tuesdays, and Wednesdays. Could that work for you?

- What if you said "no" to doing anything that did not move you forward toward your One Thing today?

- You might play with the idea of limits in your not-to-dos, like not watching more than one hour of TV, drinking no more than two cups of coffee, or being on the phone no longer than ten minutes at a time.

- Would it create more focus if you did not answer your phone today?

- How about putting multi-tasking, worrying, or complaining on your Not-To-Do List?

When we intentionally create our NOT-To-Do List, we shift ourselves out of busyness, fake work, and our old way of operating and into Zero Gravity and greatness. The practice of creating a Daily

NOT-To-Do List allows us to concentrate on activities that are more aligned with our important projects and One Thing.

Your NOT-To-Do List is flexible and can be adjusted based on each day's priorities. Just because something like not checking social media ends up on your NOT-To-Do List one day doesn't mean it has to be there tomorrow. In fact, I recommend you challenge yourself to create a completely different NOT-To-Do List every day. Taking the time to intentionally come up with new NOT-To-Dos helps you to stay vigilant and come up with ideas to make tomorrow better than today.

Your NOT-To-Do List is not just about creating another list; it's about making deliberate choices about what to avoid. This approach can lead to a more focused and less cluttered workday. When I began to incorporate the NOT-To-Do List in my Weekly Momentum session, my members found that they could achieve higher weekly productivity scores and increase their focus, especially on their One Thing. This new approach to to-do lists, focusing on both action and deliberate inaction, gave them a fresh perspective on organizing their tasks and goals. I hope you can see how it may help you create more space to be great each day.

create space to be great cheat sheet

What is work? Are we working? Are we not working? Often, if we are doing personal things, we feel guilty that we're not doing work, and when we are working, we feel guilty we are not with our friends or family. That's a very difficult game to win. If there are no clear boundaries around our time, our day all runs together. Pre-paving our day and using the tools in this part of the book allow us to time-block and plan our day in a way that gives us the space to be great.

I believe that busyness is one of the biggest labels we use to hide our greatness. We use "being busy" to avoid making choices—or so we think, but all that does is allow our environments to make our choices for us. Most of the time, we are busy because we are agreeing to things that we would be better off saying "no" to or "not right now" (like Mu did). Many times, I meet women who cannot understand why they can't stick with something to the end or they are scratching their heads wondering why they keep procrastinating instead of doing the things that are important to them. The solution may simply be taking the time to plan and pre-pave the day so that they can create the space to be great.

Download the cheat sheet for Greatness Habit Four: Create Space to Be Great, as well as the how-to videos on daily planning at
www.dailymomentumhub.com

HABIT FIVE

be consistent

"When you want more than you have, you think you need, and when you think more than you want, your thoughts begin to bleed. I think I need to find a bigger place 'cause when you have more than you think, you need more space."

—Eddie Vedder

doing great things

Carla wanted to live fully and shut down a city so that she could throw a massive party for 4,000 of her friends with her favorite bands on stage. When she did, she stepped into her greatness.

Giselle wanted to improve the quality of people's lives by making sure that educational funding went to the people who needed it the most. When she made that happen, she stepped into her greatness.

Nancy wanted her developmentally disabled daughter to live, thrive, and feel the joy of independence. When she made that happen through her own innovation, she stepped into her greatness.

Jessica wanted to move from Alaska and spend her days as a catalyst for change. When she did, she stepped into her greatness.

Kate wanted to share her powerful story of claiming her voice and writing a book, and at 72-years-young, when she did, she stepped into her greatness.

My stepmum, Tess, devoted over ten years to lovingly taking care of my dad as he declined further and further into an incurable disease. When she showed up with patience, devotion, and love and advocated again and again for his quality of life, she stepped into her greatness.

I believe greatness is realized when we start where we are, know what we want, decide to move toward it by making tomorrow better than today, and create space to be great. These amazing women made promises to themselves and followed the habits I have shared with you in this book to step into their greatness. There are examples of great men and women around us every day doing remarkable things, just like my stepmum, Tess, when she honored the promise she made in her wedding vows to my dad.

Every time we make and keep a promise to ourselves, we experience a sense of peace, order, and truth as we line up our desires and expectations with our actions. This is how we create the space for even more greatness to show up.

We have the opportunity to experience greatness hundreds of times every day. Greatness doesn't just happen at the end of the journey when the crowd is roaring and we are signing that number-one best-selling book. We can experience greatness with every single step on the journey.

Every time we choose to make a promise to ourselves that is aligned with what we truly want, we open up an opportunity for greatness. Every time we promise ourselves we will get up at 7 am and go to the gym, meditate tomorrow, or write the first chapter of our book, we are opening up an opportunity for our greatness.

If we don't deliver on our promises, as we learned earlier in the book, we make a massive deduction from our emotional bank account. Not honoring our word to ourselves opens the door to guilt, shame, regret, frustration, and even anger, and diminishes our greatness. If we are making these withdrawals even a few times a day, it can make the journey to greatness a lot steeper.

What if all the little, seemingly insignificant promises you don't keep are really what's getting in the way of you moving fully from good to great? Would you want to change that?

If you spent your life "almost being great," would that be okay?

There is a lot to be said about enjoying the journey; in fact, I believe that the journey is as important as the destination, but without a destination, there is no journey.

As high achievers, we have a call to adventure, a restlessness, and a desire to create, change, or reimagine something in the world. We know in our bones that if we had enough time, money, resources, support, energy, and faith, we could make an even bigger impact on the world. We believe in our dreams most of the time. But every time we make a withdrawal from our greatness account, it becomes even more exhausting to get up and get back in the race.

What does it take to move the dial from good to great? That's a question I have been asking for over a decade, and in our final habit of greatness, you will learn the last missing piece of the puzzle as we get into Greatness Habit Five: Be Consistent.

think big

Picture a tugboat, its vibrant colors glinting in the sun, as it cheerfully ferries tourists across the harbor. Each trip is a fun journey, from the bustling parking lot to the promise of ice cream and amusements at a seaside resort. This tugboat, guided by a captain with a clear vision, follows a set path, its course steady and true. The rudder, a symbol of this vision, holds the course steadfast, even as unpredictable winds seek to veer it off course. With clarity of direction, the tugboat completes its journey successfully, much to the delight of its passengers.

Now, imagine this same tugboat but without a defined course. It picks up eager tourists, their hearts set on sweet treats, but this time, the absence of vision leaves the boat adrift. Aimlessly, it spins in the harbor, the excitement of the tourists dimming as it spins in endless circles. Drifting consumes more and more energy and eventually, the tugboat runs out of fuel.

Going nowhere eventually wears you out. Vision steers us toward our goals, projects, and how we spend our days. Without it, we expend just as much effort but end up feeling frustrated, exhausted, and unaccomplished at the end of each day.

The majority of this book has focused on your vision of each day and your daily planning. I have shown you tools which, in the final section of this book, you will pull together to create your own habit of Daily Momentum. I have found that if we can own our day, we create more space to be great in. This then gives us the capacity to pre-pave even further ahead, gradually creating more and more spaciousness in our lives. As we embrace the final habit of greatness, Think BIG, Start Small, and Be Consistent, I am going to invite you to think a little bigger. To do that, we will use a series of questions to activate your big thinking.

The Reboot Worksheet is a powerful tool designed for deep introspection and clarification of our desires. It isn't a daily checklist but more of a compass to use at the beginning of a project, monthly or maybe weekly. Using just a handful of questions to encourage us, we can think big and tune into our greatness to ensure our rudder is pointing in the right direction.

The Reboot Questions

What do I want?

By now, you are very familiar with this question. We have asked it many times throughout the book. However, this time, I want you to think bigger as you ask it. Reflect on your desires without the constraints of time. Think beyond today and the reality you are currently operating in. For example, you might be working a nine-to-five job but what you really want is to start a business or learn a new skill to enable you to shift to a different position or industry completely.

Why is this important to me?

Understand the driving force behind your goals. Maybe starting a business represents financial freedom or learning a new skill fulfills a lifelong passion.

Who will I be after achieving this?

Envision the transformed version of yourself. Achieving a goal might mean becoming more confident, knowledgeable, or fulfilled.

What do I need to figure out to move forward?

Identify the steps, resources, or knowledge required. This could involve researching, networking, or developing a detailed plan.

What are my top three most important projects right now?

Our time and energy are finite. By pausing and identifying our top three projects, we can direct our resources to where they can make the most meaningful difference. This is not an exercise in prioritization. The question, "What are your top three most important projects right now?" is pivotal for recognizing and aligning with great work in your personal and professional life. The question challenges us to pause and recognize, in no particular order, the top three projects that resonate deeply with what we want and our One Thing. You will be using this simple list in your Daily Momentum practice to help you Think BIG, Start Small, and Be Consistent each day.

All the questions in this worksheet support you in stepping into your vision. They are focused on exploration, not immediate commitment. Maybe create a habit of asking them every thirty days to remind yourself to think BIG and stay future-focused, so you aren't spinning in circles wasting your resources of time, money, and energy.

start small

What is your Next Action Step? If you spend any amount of time with me, you are going to hear me ask that question. And I will keep asking you because I believe that defining your Next Action Step is one of the easiest ways to get into action without pushing or coercing yourself.

I was first introduced to the idea of the Next Action Step in the book *Getting Things Done* by David Allen. Allen has created a whole system for getting things done, and his concept of the Next Action Step is brilliant and powerful.

Even once we get clear on the vision of what we want, we may spend days, weeks, or even months spinning our wheels because we don't know what to do. It's like our car is just sitting in the driveway waiting to go on a really great trip but we aren't even in the car. We think we are ready: we are energized, we are excited, and perhaps we even have all the resources we need. And yet, we don't move forward. Why?

We may ask ourselves if it is because of the fear of success or perhaps the fear of failure. But all that does is invite shame, frustration, guilt, and confusion to show up. Usually, we can alleviate all this pressure by thinking small—really small—and simply defining a Next Action Step instead of needing to know the whole plan before we get started. We don't always have to have a detailed blueprint to get to our destination. Sometimes we can just start with a Next Action Step and see where it takes us next.

Taking a few minutes to identify our Next Action Step may allow us to start the car and get the engine running. I love to think of Next Action Steps as one of those ignition keys for a car, where you push a button, and even before you get in the car, it starts the engine and turns on the seat warmer. It's magic.

Defining Your Next Action Step

To begin, identify a goal, project, or One Thing that you want to add some momentum to.

Then ask yourself, "What is the next action that I could take?"

Now, your itty-bitty-shitty committee is going to have a lot to say about this, like, "That's ridiculous!" "What a waste of my time." If you're a high-achieving action taker, you may need to give yourself some time to learn from experience how potent this simple step can be before you can fully embrace it.

I know this seems so simple and obvious but stay with me here. The Next Action Step you define needs to be really small. In fact, it will be so small that you will feel silly writing it down. To help you see how small, think of it this way: your Next Action Step should take two to three minutes or less to complete. That's it!

We might set a big goal for the year; however, we may not get to taking action on that particular goal for another week or maybe another month. When we set our goals, it really helps if we write down the Next Action Step at the same time. Even if we are not going to take the step for a week or so, humor me and get into the habit of writing down your Next Action Step.

When you do, you are using your magic key to start your ignition now, without even realizing it. Your mind will start cooking up ideas like a crockpot in the background. Suddenly, you will notice resources and answers just showing up out of the blue. Magic happens.

When we write down Next Action Steps that are too big, the magic isn't quite as magical. For example, let's say one of my projects is to get better at sending out thank-you notes to people. If I want to send out ninety notes over the next ninety days, my next action step might be to go online, find some really great cards, and order them. Because I've written that down, the next time I'm online or at the grocery store, I could suddenly stumble across the perfect cards.

I love a good plan, but we don't always have to figure out every single step. Sometimes, all we need is the first one to get started.

If our goal is to lose twenty pounds or write a book, we may feel so completely overwhelmed that we can't get started. Once we start applying the idea of small steps, everything changes. Our Next Action Step might be to text a friend to ask them where they work out or see if they will be our accountability buddy.

Once we start taking Next Action Steps, we will notice synchronicity kicking in. Maybe someone will come to us with a great referral for a website designer, a free gym membership offer, or hand us a magazine article on how to write a book. We might even find ourselves taking our Next Action Step without even realizing it. That's how powerful this tool is; it gets us moving into greatness.

How do we move forward or get any momentum from just taking three minutes of action? In most cases, three minutes of action is not going to complete the project. Three minutes of action will not drop twenty pounds off your body or allow you to write an entire book. But if every time we complete our Next Action Step we write down the *next* Next Action Step, before we know it, we will have arrived at our destination. The trick is to write your Next Action Step down before you move on to the next project, go have dinner, or go to bed—even though you are not going to take it right then and there because in that moment, your Next Action Step will be clearer than at any other time. Just write it down and set the wheels in motion.

Think of your Next Action Step like warming up your car before you head out on a cold winter morning. When we define the most ridiculously small Next Action Step, we have laser clarity on exactly what needs to be done next. Maybe use a post-it note so that you can easily update your Next Action Step anytime. If it's a bright and cheerful color, it will stand out and quickly grab your attention, making it easy to jump right back in where you left off.

Most of the time, we think too big about our actions, whether it's a project or a to-do. We take too big of a chunk at a time. At first, we may feel excited, but when we're not quite sure how to get started, this stalls our progress and curbs our enthusiasm. If we don't know how to begin something, it can leave us spinning our wheels. Just having to come up with a small step, like your Next Action Step, forces you to invest time in getting crystal clear. One trick to help you get clear on your Next Action Step is to imagine you are delegating it to someone else. What would be the very first thing you would have them do? They wouldn't know how to do it like you do. You would have to be very clear and specific.

As you begin to use this tool, you may find yourself receiving support in unexpected ways. Joseph Campbell, the renowned mythologist and writer, famously wrote of having "a thousand helping hands" guiding us toward greatness. Campbell's work, deeply rooted in the power of myth and story, suggests that we're often aided by unseen forces in our journey, maybe even magic—especially when we commit to gradual, steady progress.

the vicious spin cycle

The Vicious Spin Cycle of Greatness is a two-way street: we can own our greatness and move forward toward what we want, or we can move backward when we focus on what we don't want. The choice is ours. We are taught to believe we must work hard to succeed. I am about to challenge that notion. Busyness can often simply be a smoke screen that gives us a false sense of security and instead causes backward, not forward, momentum. Let me officially introduce you to the Vicious Spin Cycle.

There is a Vicious Spin Cycle high achievers can easily fall into that pushes them backward into so much action that it makes them too busy to succeed. I know this cycle well.

Most of the people I coach feel like they need to DO more. Often, they see "the path" to greatness, success, and productivity as paved with taking more action, consuming more information, and having more ideas. It seems like that would make sense. If we want to get somewhere quicker, we take more action, get more information, and think of more ideas to get there. However, anytime we are focused on a deficit, we are in scarcity mode. Scarcity lives firmly in the lower end of the Emotional Thermometer.

Even if we do fire ourselves up and get into action, scarcity-driven action is not sustainable; all it does is burn us out. If we are not on the higher end of the Emotional Thermometer when we are planning what to do or even what we want, often we end up going down the path of backward instead of forward momentum. The most common result of action, information, and idea binging is that we end up wasting money, time, and energy getting nowhere and burning ourselves out.

When we binge on action and feel like we are not making progress, we have no sense of accomplishment. This then activates our fears and doubts and increases feelings of overwhelm. After we have rushed, pushed, and coerced ourselves forward, we may very well end up feeling more stuck and even stupid and not good enough. Which then leads us right back into the Vicious Spin Cycle again and again and again. We push ourselves forward with another burst of action, information, and idea-binging, and it's a never-ending merry-go-round going nowhere.

Backward Momentum

When we rush and push our way into anything from a place of scarcity, desperation, or fear, we shift away from our greatness into backward momentum. Approaching goals, projects, or life this way means we only see a very narrow path forward, almost as if we have tunnel vision. We can only glimpse a small crack of what is actually possible instead of seeing the whole picture.

When we are looking at life with tunnel vision, we can become so fixated on the only option we think we can see that we tend to double down and binge on action. This eventually leads to varying degrees of burnout without completing the project or hitting our goal.

I have a feeling you may be familiar with the seductive power of this Vicious Spin Cycle and perhaps have fallen into it before.

This Vicious Spin Cycle spits us out like a piece of trash. As we pick ourselves up off the floor, burned out and deflated, we often re-activate our fears, doubts, and feelings of being stuck, stupid, and not good enough. This throws us back into the Vicious Spin Cycle for another round. This is a deadly game. We all know victims of its lure. Every round sucks more of the life, energy, and passion out of us until we give up on our dreams, projects, goals, or even life itself.

Desperation is simply passion on steroids. It is the cliche boyfriend who loves you so much that he clings to you or the employee who wants the promotion so badly they are just too attentive and it turns you off. I know it may feel hard to admit that you have approached anything from a place of scarcity and desperation, but let's take a look at how simple it is for high achievers to fall into the Vicious Spin Cycle.

The Vicious Spin Cycle

PHASE ONE: Desperation is actually just passion on steroids.

It all begins with what feels like a brilliant idea. I want to make money online. I want to start a business. I want to lose weight and get healthy.

PHASE TWO: Tunnel Vision

We have a sense of scarcity, so we feel rushed and pushed into taking action toward our brilliant idea to get results as quickly as possible. I'm going to stop eating sugar. I'm going to buy that course, book, or sign up for that school.

PHASE THREE: Binging

We binge. We take lots of action all at the same time and then no action at all.

I am going to shoot videos, build a website, go to the gym every day, and write a book.

Then we spin ourselves around to phase one again. Again, and again and again...

Passion, vision, and action can be a healthy, natural flow, but it all depends on how we enter the cycle. Let me show you how to reframe your approach to this same cycle differently so that you can allow your passion, vision, and action to work for you instead of against you.

The Success Equation

PHASE ONE: Instead of feeling desperate with PASSION on steroids, find your sense of EXCITEMENT.

Start where you are and get yourself into a more satisfied state. You can use the tools you have learned so far in the book to support you in shifting your energy into your Zone of Greatness (level 7 and above on the Emotional Thermometer). When you do that, you enter the cycle with pure passion, excitement, and positive expectations instead of desperation.

PHASE TWO: Tunnel VISION turns into Eagle VISION

Because you entered the cycle from a place of satisfaction, you are more open to ideas, your creativity has space to thrive, and you don't feel rushed, so you can take the time to ask lots of questions and get clear about what you want before you take action.

PHASE THREE: ACTION-Binging becomes Consistent AC-TION

This is where the magic of steady, regular action comes into play. Instead of sporadic bursts of effort, you start to integrate small, consistent actions into your daily routine. This approach is not about grand gestures or monumental tasks; it's about the power of small, manageable steps taken regularly. By doing so, you build momentum, create habits, and foster a sense of progress that is both sustainable and effective. Consistent action is the key to turning short-term successes into long-term achievements, ensuring that your journey toward your goals is steady and uninterrupted.

We can choose to replace the Vicious Spin Cycle with the Success Equation.

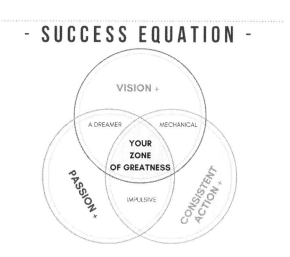

Now that you have been introduced to the Success Equation, let's dive more into the idea of Consistent Action.

the magic pill

In all areas of our lives, consistency is a necessary component of success. It's like the glue holding our vision and passion together. Many people try to compensate for a lack of time with sporadic action binges, taking lots of action and then doing nothing. These spurts of sometimes manic action seem productive yet yield few long-term results.

Many of the books out there on productivity focus on vision but leave the reader with nothing but positive thinking, a vision board, and, if they are lucky, some kind of plan to reach their destination.

Greatness is showing up every day, not just now and again. I believe everyone, me included, can benefit from more consistency in our actions and lives. Consistent action is the path to greatness. It is how we rise higher, continue to grow, and maintain a healthy balance in our lives. It is how we can stick around long enough to impact more people as we shine our greatness.

Many people who come to me for coaching tend to start a lot of new projects and then move on to another project before finishing any of them. This gives them the illusion that they are taking action, but when we start to examine what consistent action looks like and evaluate what they are doing, they quickly realize their definition of action is flawed. What they are really doing is action-binging.

Action-binging is a common trait of high achievers because we are so passionate about our ideas. But without the feeling of accomplishment that shows up when we finish projects, negative emotions—especially desperation—can set in. This leads to a craving for accomplishment and success, and so we start more projects. Starting projects and checking off items on never-ending, pointless to-do lists can be like a drug giving us a quick fix.

Do you know what is addictive? The rush of working your butt off to get something done right down to the wire and nailing it just in time! ...and heroin!

A surge of adrenaline can sometimes be confused with making progress.

If we feel overwhelmed by too many unfinished projects, then we may force, push, and coerce ourselves into more action. If we are not on the higher end of the Emotional Thermometer, then our greatness pushes back. Like the gears on a car, we screech, drag, and burn ourselves out.

Wouldn't it be great if there was a magic pill to this conundrum? Although we may not always want to admit it, consistent action is the magic pill to success in any area of our lives. If we want to lose or gain weight, consistently making different food choices and consistently expending more energy is how we will get to our desired weight. Consistently practicing our scales on the piano is the only way to improve our piano skills.

Consistent action is the magic pill! Binge action, much like binge eating or drinking, feels great when we are doing it and then gives us a really bad hangover. And after we burn out on action, the pendulum swings in the other direction, and we binge on doing nothing, with our heads buried in the sand. All this swinging actually moves us backward even further, not forward. It feels like momentum, but it's not. So, whether we are doing everything at once or nothing at all, we are moving away from greatness and further into the Vicious Spin Cycle.

If you were to pick a few things and do them consistently, in most cases, you would outperform your competition. Whether it is writing, working out, networking, going to bed on time, or planning your day, consistency is key. And just like the tugboat in the success equation, you will take the same amount of fuel.

You see, spinning in circles for a mile or going on a leisurely one-mile stroll takes the same amount of energy. Consistency helps you cover more ground, forging you forward without binging and burning you out.

stay consistent

Sally opened her own photography business about two years ago. She was well-trained and confident in her skills. Yet, it made her crazy to see how bad some photographers in her industry were. She couldn't understand how they were doing so well and getting so many clients when their photos were so bad. Sally would see their flyers, ads, postcards, and cheesy pictures everywhere; they haunted her. Why was it that she did such a great job, yet her business was struggling?

Sally shot newborns, headshots, families and weddings, anything really. And her bank account was empty. While sitting in desperation with another stack of bills to pay, Sally had an idea. "I will target event planners so that I can get them to refer their wedding clients to me!"

Quickly, with the same attention to detail and creative flair that Sally brought to her photography, she began to create little gifts for the event planners: high-quality chocolates in just the right box wrapped up with a beautiful bow and a stunning flier about her wedding packages. She sweated over every word with incredible attention to detail, pulling an all-nighter until it was done.

The next day, she excitedly delivered the beautiful gifts to 25 local event planners. Some she met and got to surprise and delight; others she dropped off, and one refused the gift with a callus wave of their hand. "No soliciting," they said.

Sally knew that following up was important, so after waiting for three days, she picked up the phone and began calling each of the event planners one by one to see if they had received their gift. After several hours of, "Yes, thank you. Who is this?" and leaving voicemails, she was done.

Then she waited and waited for the phone to ring. Not one return phone call. Two weeks, three weeks, six months...not one of the event planners called or sent her a referral. That's when Sally called me.

It takes 25 to 28 interactions with someone on average before they buy—or, in this case, refer someone to you. It takes consistent action to get to that point, not sporadic or erratic action and all-nighters.

First, Sally and I got clear on what she was PASSIONATE about and what she wanted to shoot. When we did, it was very clear that weddings were not profitable or really that much fun for her. Instead, she enjoyed newborns and families, so we ditched the event planner strategy and began to CONSISTENTLY talk about family photography so that potential clients could clearly understand what she had to offer.

We went through her pricing so that she could be confident and consistent with what she was charging. We picked out three simple marketing strategies as well as nailing down a follow-up process that felt fun and authentic to her.

It wasn't instant; however, after a year, there was a consistent stream of new clients coming to her! The new clients that came in were a perfect fit because her marketing message was consistent. Follow-up was now an art, and Sally enjoyed getting to chat on the phone and check in with her clients. Wedding referrals were delightfully passed along to someone else, and although it was scary at first to turn down clients, within a year, her income had doubled. She took on a virtual assistant to upgrade her follow-up procedures even more.

One day, as Sally was moving some boxes in the garage, she came across some of those pretty boxes she had bought to put the chocolates in. She smiled to herself and enjoyed a wave of appreciation for how far she had come.

Action-Binging

Action-binging comes in all shapes and sizes.

It happens when we are desperate and feel stuck or when we are desperately seeking approval to fill the hole caused by something important missing in our personal or professional lives.

- We go to the gym seven days a week then don't go again for six months.

- We write five blog articles in a month then none for a year.

- We post on social media dozens of times a day then disappear for months.

- We talk about a different hobby or idea every month and don't master any of them.

- We make ten phone calls in one day then go months without picking up the phone again.

- We send out cards to everyone we know over the holidays and then never call or check in with most people for the rest of the year.

- We try to be everything to everyone and end up being nothing to anyone.

Consistent action sends a loud message: I am here, I am committed, and I am ready to receive.

The funny thing is, often the results may come from a different direction than you expect. Consistent action allows you to feel more confident and calmer about what you are doing, and that attracts opportunities to you like a magnet.

Consistency is also about how you do what you do. It is reflected in the quality of the work you do and keeping your standards at the same level every single time. Consistency is not just about showing up; it's about bringing your greatness, day in and day out, to a few things rather than mediocrity to many. Consistency in quality is what makes you reliable, trustworthy, and a cut above the rest. It's doing things well, every time, without fail.

If you are a professional, your message needs to be repeated the same way again and again to make an impact. If you change your thirty-second pitch every single time you go to a networking event, there is no consistency. People need repetition to build trust in who you are and what you do.

Consistency also comes into play in how you deliver great work. You create expectations, especially for repeat customers. If you are not consistent with how you show up for work, these expectations cannot be met.

Even branding is improved with consistency. Notice how your favorite brands always have their logo in the same spot, use the same tagline in their email signature and on their website, and are consistent with the colors and messaging about their products, all to help their customers know, like, and trust their brand.

It may seem like successful people have a higher skill level, better connection, a gift, or a special talent. However, most of the time, if you really look, you will find that their secret weapon is consistency. Great people show up consistently to practice, rehearse, and train. They fail often and grow through consistency. Momentum gets you started; consistency gets you across the finish line.

key performance indicators

Hot yoga class number one was hell! Class number 99 was back aching, and number 182 was my best class ever. I know now from experience that no matter how consistent I am with my hot yoga practice, my results will vary. So, I can expect more hell, more back aching, and more best classes ever in the future.

Just when I think I'm not making any progress or even feel like I am moving backward, out of nowhere, a breakthrough shows up! I find myself lifting my legs a little higher, balancing longer, or opening up my chest even deeper.

My body has spent over four decades with a tight chest, unsteady balance, and inflexibility. Showing up and going through the motions of the 26 postures and two breathing exercises of hot yoga almost every day often feels like I am attempting to move through concrete. Yet, even concrete can be penetrated by something as gentle and beautiful as a flower. But only if that flower is consistent.

In yoga class, during the standing series, there is a pose called Standing Head to Knee. Every day, as I step into the pose, the instructor says the same words to the class. "Just pick up your foot, don't think. Just pick up your foot."

When I don't feel like going to class, I just pick up my foot and get in the car. When I'm writing a book and I'm not in the mood, I just pick up my foot and start typing. And when no one has signed up for my new workshop and I feel like throwing in the towel, I just pick up my foot anyway and show up. Don't get me wrong—I am not pushing or coercing myself to take action that is not aligned with my passion. I'm just pointing out that not every day is going to feel easy. That's normal. But how do you get through it? With non-negotiables and Key Performance Indicators.

Gold medal athletes have things in their life that are simply non-negotiable. It might be swimming thirty laps daily so that their stamina never has the opportunity to dwindle or not eating two hours before they swim because it slows them down.

Like dominos, just one non-negotiable can trigger dozens of actions almost effortlessly. When I started doing hot yoga every day, before I knew it, laundry was being done daily (instead of just when I ran out of clothes) for all the sweaty towels and clothes. I was showering (and shaving my legs!!) daily. I drank extra water so that I had energy and remained hydrated during class. I ate more regularly and refueled with foods that gave me energy but didn't sit in my stomach. I became a scientist of what effects sleep, food, activities during the day, and different variables had on my performance each day in hot yoga. I was tuning into what made me great and motivated to make upgrades.

Then one day, as I got in the car to go to yoga, I realized that hot yoga every day had become a non-negotiable for me. I hadn't pushed myself to do it; it just was. It's funny; I have no desire to be an athlete and have never shown interest in sports or sporting competition in my life before, and here I was, acting like an athlete. Instead of using willpower, what I had unconsciously done was upgrade my defaults by adopting new non-negotiables!

Once we consciously decide to raise our standards by putting in place non-negotiables, consistent commitment to them is what will upgrade us to a new level of greatness. Consistency gives us an edge so that we can break through old behaviors and conquer new challenges to win the gold medal. Being consistent with anything can make us feel proud, accomplished, invigorated, and happy. And yet, consistency can also feel boring, pointless, painful, and even demoralizing at times. If we want to stay consistent through these ups and downs, we need to find fun ways to measure and track our progress.

Key Performance Indicators are one way we can measure our consistency and work particularly well to measure our non-negotiables. Key Performance Indicators gamify consistent action and make it much more fun, even on those days when it feels difficult or even painful to show up and keep doing what we are doing! Key Performance Indicators help us stay in the race and celebrate our consistent action, even when we are not seeing the results we want yet. They are a tool to help us feel a sense of accomplishment and measure progress so that we can keep picking up our foot when our lack of results may leave us feeling like we want to throw in the towel.

In business, Key Performance Indicators (KPIs) are quantifiable measures that gauge a company's performance against its specific objectives. They provide a clear picture of whether a business is on track to achieve its targeted goals. KPIs are the navigational tools that help steer a business toward success, offering insights into areas of progress and those needing improvement. Essentially, they are vital signposts on the road to achieving business milestones.

> **Key Performance Indicators** (KPIs) are metrics that
> help us track our progress toward
> personal or professional goals and objectives.

Key Performance Indicator Examples

Health and Fitness KPIs:

- Number of weekly workout sessions

- Daily step count or distance ran/walked

- Consistency in maintaining a healthy diet

- Hours of quality sleep per night

Financial KPIs:

- Monthly savings as a percentage of income

- Reduction in unnecessary expenditures

- Credit score improvement

- Investment portfolio growth

Professional Development KPIs:

- Number of professional training or courses completed

- Quarterly performance reviews and feedback

- Number of new skills acquired

- Progression toward a promotion or career milestone

Personal Development KPIs:

- Books read per month

- Time spent on hobbies or personal interests

- Frequency of practicing mindfulness or meditation

- Engagement in community service or volunteer work

Relationships and Social KPIs:

- Quality time spent with family and friends

- Number of meaningful conversations per week

- Participation in social or community events

- Frequency of expressing gratitude or appreciation to loved ones

KPIs can be tailored to fit our goals and aspirations, providing a measurable way to track progress in various aspects of our personal or professional lives. They give us a way to enjoy a sense of accomplishment along the way at each mile-marker, not just when we cross the finish line.

KPIs can be the rhythm we move to. They can be the pulse that keeps our actions consistent and aligns us with our goals, dreams, and One Thing. KPIs are like the beats in a song that guide our steps, ensuring we dance in tune with our objectives. They help us measure progress, fine-tune our strategies, and stay on track.

A car has a dashboard to give constant feedback to the driver about speed, direction, and even how far away from our destination we are. Tracking KPIs gives us that same constant feedback so that we can make sure our actions are driving us where we want to go.

How do you measure greatness? In the next chapter, I am going to give you six key metrics you can use to design your own KPIs and track your progress at the end of every day.

metrics of greatness

I have created a little game with a scorecard that I use daily to help me and the members of the Momentum Squad define Key Performance Metrics and track our progress in a very simple and satisfying way. It's called the Daily Satisfaction Quiz. It's much more fun than a spreadsheet. It allows us to quickly see what's working, what's not, and why it's more accurate than if we just depend on our memory.

Regular tracking of our KPIs allows us to see where there is room for growth and to notice what we want more and less of. This simple Daily Satisfaction Quiz is also a great way to keep our expectations in check. Remember, I earlier mentioned that successful results are created when we align our intentions and our expectations so that they move us forward together rather than pulling us in different directions.

When my clients use the Daily Satisfaction Quiz to regularly track their progress, 90% of the time, they realize they are getting way more done than they realized. When we recognize our WINS and the progress we are making, we move into our Zone of Greatness, and this continues in an upward swing that requires very little energy to maintain. Momentum!

In this chapter, you are going to learn how to create a habit of checking in and receiving feedback on your productivity and satisfaction each day using the Daily Satisfaction Quiz.

This ridiculously simple quiz will only take you five to ten seconds to complete each day. Doable, right? I hope so because the benefits of this little quiz are exponential!

The Daily Productivity Quiz will measure your satisfaction and productivity using the Six Areas of Satisfaction.

Six Areas of Satisfaction

ACCOMPLISHMENT | That amazing feeling of being productive, proud, or having challenged yourself is so delightful. When scoring this area, reflect on the projects and tasks you set out to do that day and how good you were at finishing things.

SPACE | When we don't feel rushed and pushed into doing things. It's when we have a sense of spaciousness, like there is more than enough time and physical space for us to be creative and enjoy what we are doing in the moment.

As you decide on your score for this area, think about how you moved through the day. Did you rush and push or did you have room to breathe?

PROGRESS | When we feel like we are moving forward toward our goals or projects. To score this area, zoom out a little or a lot beyond today. Think about your One Thing or longer-term goals. How did you move forward toward your goals today?

FOCUS | Happens when we are able to devote time to our projects and goals without being distracted, overwhelmed, or procrastinating. It's when we are in the Zone of Greatness!

When scoring this area, evaluate if you had any uninterrupted time to focus on your One Thing today. Did you operate in your Zone of Greatness or complete any Power Hours today?

FREEDOM | Feels like we have a choice to focus on whatever we want, whenever we want. This score depends on feeling like you could do whatever you wanted today—even when you are on someone else's clock. It might mean how you do things, not just what you do.

FUN | Happens when we feel happy, connected to others, and feel like we are learning and growing. We are wired to learn; when we don't feel this way, we feel lost and without a purpose. Score yourself on how much laughter, learning, or leisure you had today.

The Daily Satisfaction Quiz

All we have to do to leverage the power of the Daily Satisfaction Quiz is to grade ourselves from 1–5 in each of the Six Areas of Satisfaction at the end of each day.

- A score of 1 would mean not at all satisfied.

- A score of 5 would indicate extremely satisfied.

This powerful little quiz looks at our level of satisfaction in all six areas to give us a total score. We can track that number daily. If you prefer to see things as a percentage, you can add up your score and then divide it by .03 to get your daily percentage instead.

The better you understand the Six Areas of Satisfaction and your expectations around them each day, the more likely you are to feel satisfied at the end of each day. To help you develop a better understanding of how this works, you can use the questions below as journal prompts to use at the beginning of each day. By asking these questions in the morning, you will pre-pave a better score at the end of each day. I am also giving you some examples to give you a little inspiration on how to answer each of the prompts.

ACCOMPLISHMENT

- What would I like to finish by the end of the day?

- What might accomplishment look like for me today?

- What three things could I accomplish today?

Example: Get my nails done. Run payroll. Take care of client's monthly bookkeeping. Pick up a rental car. Take the car in for service. Prep the turkey.

SPACE

- How can I create a "Winning Environment" today?

- What do I need to allow time for today?

- How can I create more ease and flow today?

Example: Shower time, not just zipping in and out. Buffer time built in between appointments. Finish appointments on time by setting a timer 15 minutes before the end of each appointment. Organize my day in the morning.

PROGRESS

- What steps can I take today toward my bigger goals and projects?

- How will today's efforts impact my future?

- How will I measure my success today?

Example: If **I c**alled the care agency to hire someone. If a new employee is trained and ready to go out on her own.

FOCUS

- When is my "Power Hour" today?

- What things require my undivided attention today?

- How can I minimize distractions today?

Examples: Ask for privacy so that I can talk freely with my client with fewer distractions. Set up a Power Hour for 10 am. Not go on social media till 6 pm.

FREEDOM

- When is my free time today (when I can do whatever I want)?

- Is there anything I can release control of today and instead allow it to happen in a new or different way?

- How can I shift my schedule today to create more breathing room and less rushing?

Examples: Free time in the evening from 7 pm to 9: 30 pm. Walk to pick up the rental car. Set timers for meetings to release my responsibility to watch the clock.

FUN

- What feels fun about today?

- How will I play today?

- What can I do for self-care today?

Example: Getting my nails done. My private coaching session. Listening to two chapters of my mystery book.

The Satisfaction Challenge

Satisfaction is an easy way to quickly indicate if we are in the neighborhood of our greatness or not. If we notice that our day was not as satisfying as we'd like it to be, we can ask ourselves questions to identify how to get into our Zone of Greatness. Questions like, "What would have made my fun score a four instead of a three today?" will get us thinking and help us come up with do-overs we can use in our Daily Do-Over.

As we do this, we develop our palate for more satisfying things and what we want more and less of in our lives that can become a blueprint mapping out how we can operate more often in our Zone of Greatness in the future.

Every day is different with different experiences and variables, so the Daily Satisfaction Quiz is fresh and new each day. Just repeating everything from one day to the next will not guarantee you a winning score. You need to be creative to win the game of satisfaction on a consistent basis. And as you do, you will be priming the pump for consistency in more areas of your personal and professional life.

Often, the days that are the most satisfying are also quite productive, but usually only if there is variety within our days. The six elements of satisfaction give us six different metrics to watch to help us bring in all flavors of satisfaction every day.

Simply completing this quick quiz at the end of each day alone for thirty days will create change without you consciously deciding to change anything. The Daily Satisfaction Quiz activates our natural curiosity and creates a sense of fun by making a game out of greatness. This enables us to measure something that is often intangible in a more concrete way.

Let me give you a couple of tips to help you create a habit of completing the Daily Satisfaction Quiz every day. Yep, even on weekends. Every day!

First, I want you to set up a recurring appointment on your phone to take the quiz at the end of each day. Not the end of your work day—the end of your day, before you go to bed.

This brings me to an important distinction. This book is inviting you to upgrade your greatness in ALL areas of your life, not just your professional life. Often, clients come to work with me and forget to include their WHOLE life in the process. When you are asking yourself the questions in the Daily Satisfaction Quiz, answer them for your day as a whole, not just the "work" part of it. Otherwise, you will upgrade your work and the other areas of your life will lag.

Back to the daily recurring appointment on your phone. I have created an easy way for you to take the quiz online. It even adds up your score and gives you a daily percentage.

**You can take the Daily Satisfaction Quiz
at www.dailymomentumhub.com**

When you make the recurring appointment, here is a critical step—don't skip this. Add the link to take the quiz in the notes, URL, or location section of the appointment. That way, when it pops up to remind you to take the quiz each day, you don't have to go searching for the link. You can simply click, take the quiz, and ten seconds later go back to what you were doing. Even if you are still out and about, just take the quiz when it pops up. Don't silence or snooze it and think you will remember to take it later. Chances are you won't.

My final tip is to record your daily score. An easy way to do this is to take a screenshot on your phone at the end of the quiz when it shows you your score. Your phone will automatically note the date for you, and you can easily pull your scores back up to review them.

If you already have one of my Momentum Planners, I suggest you write your daily score on the weekly page at the top in the white area above each day. Seeing the scores for the week will allow you to see patterns so that you can begin to notice what factors are influencing your score each day.

be consistent
cheat sheet

Big vision is a great way to pre-pave the future we see in our imagination, and if we back it up with the magic pill of consistency, we will make progress much more quickly toward our goals. When we combine our passion (what we truly want) with vision and consistent action, this then creates a powerful tri factor I like to call the Success Equation.

The burst of energy we feel when a brilliant idea first pops into our head can give us a rush. Michael Gerber has coined the term "entrepreneurial seizure" to describe how it feels when we get a great business idea in his book *The E-Myth Revisited*. But how do we keep our momentum flowing beyond the initial rush at the beginning of any idea, project, or goal? In this section of the book, I shared with you the concepts of non-negotiables and Key Performance

Indicators (KPIs) as tools to help you measure your progress daily or weekly and stay in momentum.

The best way to bring all these ideas together is to put them into a one or two-page plan. Then use that plan to gamify your approach to projects, goals, and vision for the future you want to create. The best plans contain all three elements of the Success Equation and KPIs to enable you to clearly see your milestones and track your progress toward your end goal.

Behind every great woman (or man) is a great plan! Over the last two decades, I have created hundreds of plans with clients and members, and my absolute favorite is a Ninety-Day Power Plan. I believe that ninety days is the sweet spot in planning. It feels far enough in the future for us to imagine a different reality being possible and enough time to create changes without rushing, pushing, or burning out.

The Momentum Squad is the mastermind community I created for smart, ambitious, high-achieving women who want to use Ninety-Day Planning and weekly check-ins to Think Big, Start Small, and Be Consistent toward their goals. If you would like to find out more and create your next Ninety-Day Power Plan with me, go to www.getitdonediva.me/join.

As we reach the end of this section, Think BIG, Start Small, and Be Consistent, the moment you've been waiting for is just around the corner. In the next chapter, I will guide you through integrating all the habits and tools we have learned into your own Daily Momentum Practice.

You can download the cheat sheet for Greatness Habit Five: Be Consistent, access the Daily Satisfaction Quiz, and find out more about my Momentum Planners at www.dailymomentumhub.com

Up next, create your own Daily Momentum Practice, turning theory into a daily ritual that will energize and inspire you. Get ready to see how all these pieces fit together seamlessly in your everyday life!

your daily
momentum habit

"It's a beautiful day. Don't let it get away. It's a beautiful day."

—U2

4 days

It all began after attending my best friend's birthday party when my car wouldn't start. It took not one, not two, but three tow trucks to transport my car to the mechanic. As a result, I found myself stranded in LA for a total of four days, but boy did those days turn into an adventure!

I got to stay on two different awesome friends' couches, embracing the freedom and joy of the situation. Every moment became an opportunity to connect with old friends, explore the city, and enjoy the incredible hospitality of my loved ones.

Amidst all the disruption and excitement, I managed to keep my business running smoothly without missing a beat. I facilitated Weekly Momentum for my Momentum Squad members, received and processed orders for planners, coached clients during VIP days, and kept myself and my business running on all four cylinders. All of this was thanks to the Five Habits of Greatness and the tools I have shared with you so far in this book. With each roadblock, change, or dead-end I encountered, I used my Daily Momentum practice to navigate my way through.

It was four days, three tow trucks, two couches, and one unforgettable adventure.

Over the last 18 years, my Daily Momentum practice has helped me turn all my experiences into gold and stay in constant momentum. Daily Momentum gives me a daily framework that steers me away from binging on action or burning out and instead moves me forward toward more ease, joy, and greatness in my work and play.

Finally, it's time for me to help you design your Daily Momentum practice. You will build your practice using many of the tools we have already covered in the book. Collectively, these tools are designed to provide clarity and direction at the start and end of each day. They encourage honest, rapid self-reflection, helping to align your daily actions with your bigger goals and projects. This simple practice will empower you to stay in motion, find opportunity in every situation, and shift from good to great, no matter what happens to disrupt your day.

I've already introduced all the tools necessary for your journey. Now, all we need to do is bring them together to form your Daily Momentum practice. This practice is divided into two key segments. The first, "Own Your Day," is designed around your morning routine, setting the tone for your day ahead. The second, "Upgrade Your Day," is intended for your evening, helping you reflect and unwind.

In this section of the book, I'll dive into the specifics of each segment.

By dedicating just 15 minutes a day to each of these daily segments, you'll start to see remarkable transformations. These small daily investments are the seeds that will grow into hours of productive time, elevating you from good to great. Get ready—your life is about to become even more exciting.

own your day

Their are twelve tools that make up your Daily Momentum practice. I like to think of them as "The Daily Dozen." If you are willing to spend a few minutes a day on just ONE of these tools you, you will create:

1. Momentum you can feel

2. Results you can see

3. And life-changing habits

Use the Daily Dozen tools as you begin each day. Develop your daily practice by building it one tool at a time or as many as you like. Schedule your day around your Own-Your-Day practice and do your best to complete it at the same time each day.

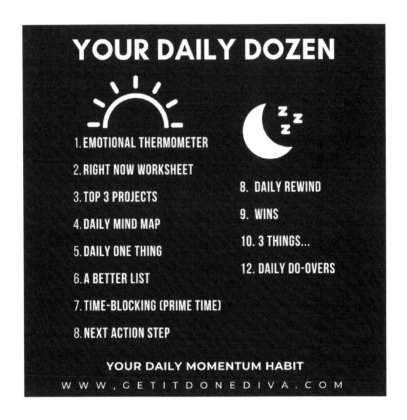

YOUR DAILY DOZEN

1. EMOTIONAL THERMOMETER
2. RIGHT NOW WORKSHEET
3. TOP 3 PROJECTS
4. DAILY MIND MAP
5. DAILY ONE THING
6. A BETTER LIST
7. TIME-BLOCKING (PRIME TIME)
8. NEXT ACTION STEP

8. DAILY REWIND
9. WINS
10. 3 THINGS...
12. DAILY DO-OVERS

YOUR DAILY MOMENTUM HABIT
W W W . G E T I T D O N E D I V A . C O M

THE OWN-YOUR-DAY PRACTICE

Your Daily Momentum practice will give you a sense of satisfaction and accomplishment when you see what you have done each day. Uninterrupted blocks of time to work on projects will make you feel like you are making progress toward your goals. You will have more confidence as you learn how to focus on what is in front of you without feeling distracted. You will be able to eliminate guilt, overwhelm, and procrastination and instead feel flow and momentum as you get more stuff done. You will create the space and freedom to do more of the things you want to do and less of the things you feel you have to do.

Daily Page 1 | START WHERE YOU ARE

The first tool we will use in your Daily Momentum practice is the Right Now Worksheet. We covered this thoroughly in the chapter titled _right now_ in the Greatness Habit Two section of the book. You will find a quick recap below. You can also revisit the _right now_ chapter anytime to brush up on this tool.

The Right Now Worksheet will get you laser-focused and ready to start your day

> **Purchase a _Daily Momentum 30 Day Planner_** with the Right Now Worksheet and all four pages of the Daily Momentum practice for thirty days at **www.thegetitdonesystem.com**

The Right Now Worksheet will get you laser-focused and ready to start your day and is a great way to begin the ritual of Daily Momentum. Use the Right Now prompts at the beginning of each day to give yourself a little boost as you start your Daily Momentum Practice.

- Right now, I feel...

- Right now, I want...

- Right now, I appreciate...

- Right now, I am having lots of fun...

- Right now, I want to eat/drink...

- Right now, it would be great if...

- Right now, I am looking forward to...

- Right now, the questions I am asking are...

Date:

Right now I feel...
Happy, like I can breathe again. Cozy. Well rested. Excited about the next book.

Right now I want...
New planner to be approved for print. Fun day laughing with Sofie. Matt's online store
ready to launch. Two more Best Selling Diva clients. Go to floating sound bath again.
Bulletproof coffee. A fun vacation with Sofie over the summer.

Right now I appreciate...
Cozy fire. Kirkfit and the whole community there. My next door neighbor best friend.
The Momentum Squad members showing up for Weekly Momentum each week.

Right now I am having lots of fun...
Upgrading the 30 Day Planner. Sharing the new book with everyone. Doing jigsaw puzzles.
Putting my Lego together. Staying home by the fire. Playing with new software.

Right now I want to eat/drink...
Bulletproof coffee. Pumpkin cheesecake. Sweet potato mashed potatoes from Hungry
Root. Mushroom coffee. Salmon and roast veggies.

Right now it would be great if...
Daily Momentum made the New York Times Best Seller List! 25 + ladies at the next
retreat. Kirk and I booked a fun cruise vacation. I found the perfect time and place to
do a book launch party. I booked a trip to Sedona. I have some camping booked.

Right now I am looking forward to...
Family beach vacation. Books and planners all upgraded, approved and selling.
Doing my new jigsaw puzzle. Weekly Momentum with the ladies. Being at the beach for
the next retreat.

Right now the questions I am asking are:

Problem/Challenge/Obstacle	Rephrased as a Question
How can I easily get shopify working for Matt?	What else is possible? Another software?
How can I connect book sales in one place?	What special Amazon programs can I set up?
When and where shall I do a book launch?	

Daily Page 2 | KNOW WHAT YOU WANT

Next, it's time to pre-pave successful outcomes for your day. To do that, we will be using the Six Areas of Satisfaction that I introduced to you in the chapter titled *metrics of greatness* in the *Greatness Habit Five* section of this book. When you take a few minutes to answer the journal prompts around each of the Six Areas of Satisfaction before you start each day, you will create more focus and clarity about exactly how you would like today to unfold.

Here are some options of how to pre-pave your day using the Six Areas of Satisfaction Worksheet to get to know what you want:

OPTION 1: Pick one of the areas from the Six Areas of Satisfaction to journal about each day of the week and revisit one on the last day of the week. Monday might be Accomplishment, Tuesday Space, etc. Then on Sunday, pick the one that feels the most fun to revisit. Answer all the journal prompts or just one each day.

OPTION 2: Select one question from each of the Six Areas of Satisfaction each day. This way, you cover all six areas every day by selecting just one journal prompt for each.

OPTION 3: Go for it! Answer all the journal prompts for all Six Areas of Satisfaction every day.

You can mix and match the above options, too, depending on how much momentum you need and how much time you want to invest in your practice each day.

Purchase a *Daily Momentum 30 Day Planner* with this worksheet and all four pages of the Daily Momentum practice for thirty days at **www.thegetitdonesystem.com**

Below, you will find a quick recap of the Six Areas of Satisfaction, including the journal prompts for each area. You can also revisit the chapter titled <u>*metrics of greatness*</u> in the *Greatness Habit Five* section of this book for a full description of this tool.

ACCOMPLISHMENT

- What would I like to finish by the end of the day?

- What might accomplishment look like for me today?

- What three things could I accomplish today?

SPACE

- How can I create a "Winning Environment" today?

- What do I need to allow time for today?

- How can I create more ease and flow today?

PROGRESS

- What steps can I take today toward my bigger goals and

projects?

- How will today's efforts impact my future?

- How will I measure my success today?

FOCUS

- When is my "Power Hour" today?

- What things require my undivided attention today?

- How can I minimize distractions today?

FREEDOM

- When is my free time today (when I can do whatever I want)?

- Is there anything I can release control of today and instead allow it to happen in a new or different way?

- How can I shift my schedule today to create more breathing room and less rushing?

FUN

- What feels fun about today?

- How will I play today?

- What can I do for self-care today?

DAILY **MOMENTUM** PAGE **2** KNOW WHAT YOU WANT

6 ELEMENTS OF SATISFACTION

ACCOMPLISHMENT:
- What would I like to finish by the end of the day?
- What might accomplishment look like for me today?
- What 5 things could I accomplish today?

1. PDF Cheat Sheets done   2. Example pages created.

3. Organize all the projects in Canva and delete old ones.   4. Do my Weekly Momentum

5. Mind Map about retreat.

SPACE:
- How could I create a "Winning Environment" today?
- What do I need to allow time for today?
- How could I create more ease and flow today?

Put laundry away. Power Hour in the AM. Take shower in the AM. and get dressed.

Time to focus on new book. Do admin first.

PROGRESS:
- What steps could I take today towards my bigger goals and projects?
- How will today's efforts impact my future?
- How will I measure my success today?

All phase I PDF's are done and uploaded.

Outline next book.

Final updates of manuscripts done.

FOCUS:
- When is my "Power Hour" today?
- What things require my undivided attention today?
- How could I minimize distractions today?

8.30 am - 9.30 am planner edits

Review manuscript at coffee shop

Wear headphones

FREEDOM:
- When is my free time today (when I can do whatever I want?
- Is there anything I could release control of today and instead allow to happen in a new or different way?
- How could I shift my schedule today to create more breathing room and less rushing?

2 pm onwards personal time.

Don't do any videos's today.

Move 3 pm appointment to 1 pm instead

FUN:
- What feels fun about today?
- How will I play today?
- What could I do for self-care today?

Being complete with manuscripts and this quarters goals and projects!

Seeing family. Doing a jigsaw puzzle.

Daily Page 3 | CREATE SPACE TO BE GREAT

Purchase a *Daily Momentum 30 Day Planner* with this
worksheet and all four pages of the Daily Momentum practice
for thirty days at **www.thegetitdonesystem.com**

Take Your Emotional Temperature

How do you feel right now? Use the Emotional Thermometer to
identify exactly how you feel. Then come up with three different
words to describe how you feel right now even more specifically.
This will help you expand your emotional vocabulary.

What's fascinating to me is that I almost always feel significantly different in this step compared to how I felt when I began my practice
and asked the exact same question when I was completing the Right
Now prompts just a few minutes before.

We learned all about taking your emotional temperature and the
Emotional Thermometer in the chapter titled *your emotional scale*,
in the *Greatness Habit One* section of this book.

The Emotional Thermometer

1 BLISS | 100°

2 PASSION | 95°

3 ENTHUSIASM | 90°

4 BELIEF | 85°

5 OPTIMISM | 80°

6 HOPE | 75°

7 SATISFACTION | 72°

8 BOREDOM | 70°

9 NEGATIVITY | 65°

10 FRUSTRATION | 60°

11 OVERWHELM | 55°

12 DISAPPOINTMENT | 50°

13 DOUBT | 45°

14 WORRY | 40°

15 BLAME | 35°

16 DISCOURAGED | 30°

17 ANGER | 25°

18 REVENGE | 20°

19 HATRED | 15°

20 JEALOUSY | 10°

21 SELF-DOUBT | 5°

22 FEAR | 0°

Top Three Projects

We covered this tool at the end of the chapter titled _think big_ in the section on _Greatness Habit Five_. These are the most important projects you are working on right now. Your Top Three Projects go beyond today, but reviewing them daily will allow you to think BIG so that you can make sure you keep moving toward them. These are projects that will most likely take you days, weeks, or months to complete. Reminding yourself of them each day keeps you focused on them so that you can stay in consistent action and steer clear of fake work, distractions, and procrastination that may get in the way of you accomplishing them. You can also use your Top Three Projects to help you create and organize your Daily To-Do List.

Daily One Thing

To focus is to put your full energy and attention on one thing. You can only focus fully on one thing at a time. Look at your schedule for today and intentionally time-block your day. Decide what it is you're going to do and when you are going to do it. As you are doing this, set a Daily One Thing to give your day clear direction and focus. Your Daily One Thing will serve as a reminder of what is most important today to help you prioritize and stay on track throughout the day.

When you decide what your Daily One Thing will be today, be open to adjusting it. As you mind map and create a Better List in the next steps of your Own Your Day process, you may decide to change it.

That's normal; just write in pencil so that you can stay up to speed with changes.

We covered daily scheduling and time blocking in the chapter titled *time-blocking* in *Greatness Habit Four*. You can remind yourself all about the One Thing tool by revisiting the chapters titled *one thing* and *what's your one thing* in the section of this book on *Greatness Habit Two*.

A Better List

Instead of having a long, never-ending to-do list and shuffling tasks from day to day in an endless, unsatisfying cycle, why not make a Better List? I introduced you to this concept in the chapter titled *a better list* in the section on *Greatness Habit Four*. A Better List is a much shorter list that you can commit to. Below is a recap of some of the steps you can use to create a Better List each day.

Mind Map

Begin each day fresh. Start with a blank plain sheet of paper so that you don't just shuffle to-dos from day to day. Draw a small circle in the middle, roughly the size of a large coin. Inside the circle write, "Where do I want to be by the end of today?" Next, draw lines out from this circle, connecting to other words in smaller circles that relate to all the things you want to accomplish, change, create, eliminate, or just get done today. Draw each one in its own circle and place it deliberately somewhere on the page. You are brainstorming, so don't limit yourself by editing what you write down. If it is in your head right now, get it down on the page. If it's a thought, then it's most likely an expectation, and if you don't acknowledge it in this step, it could hijack your day.

Cherry Pick

Identify the things you might like to include on your Daily To-Do List today. If you like, you can number them in no particular order so that they stand out on the mind map. Maybe add a star to them or highlight them.

Then count them. Keep eliminating and counting until you have five items, and then write them in any order on your Daily To-Do List in pencil. We are not done yet!

Be Realistic

Go down all the items on the list and next to each one write how long you think it will take you to complete it. If any of the to-dos will take you longer than thirty minutes, then it is likely a project, not a to-do.

Projects are made up of a series of actions. To-dos are individual tasks or very small projects that usually take less than thirty minutes to complete. Break any projects into to-dos or remove the project from the list completely and back-burner it.

Will this list fit in with the time you have today? Add up how long each item will take you to do and then look at your daily schedule.

What might you have to shift or change to make this list fit better into your day?

Pre-Pave

Once you are done, here are some more questions to help you use the concept of pre-paving to build an even Better List. I introduce the idea of pre-paving in the chapter titled *pre-pave* in the section of this book on *Greatness Habit Four*.

Look at the items on your list. Do you feel a sense of excitement or dread? If there is something on your list that you don't want to do or that feels scary, ask yourself, "How can I upgrade this item?"

If you need to complete a project for someone else that you already committed to but really aren't excited about doing, how can you shift it? Can you think of a fun place to do it rather than at your desk? Or could you find someone to do it with you or for you? Writing down "co-create new client proposal with Marcie" instead of, "work with Marcie on client proposal" may be all it takes. Sometimes all you need is to change a word, and suddenly, a to-do item feels so much more fun.

Finally, look over the list and imagine "What will this create?" How will doing these things change your life? What will be different once you have done them? If what you see in your imagination is NOT moving you forward toward what you truly want, then change the list until it is moving you toward a future that you do want. Your Daily To-Do List doesn't have to completely transform your life in one day, but it should support you in taking some small steps toward the future you want.

Prime Time

We learned all about Prime Time in the chapter titled *prime time* in the *Greatness Habit Four* section of this book. We all have approximately four and a half hours of concentrated time each day on average. Think of this as your Prime Time, the time you want to ideally spend wisely on activities and projects that will move you forward toward your goals.

Prime Time is when our mental focus, energy, and productivity are at their highest. This window varies from person to person but is typically when we are most alert and capable of producing our greatest work. Prime Time creates the space for us to be great! Look at today's schedule and make sure that you are doing your most important activities in your Prime Time. If not, move things around until you are leveraging your Prime Time as much as possible.

Next 1, 2, 3 Action Steps

Remember the power of small actions? We covered the tool Next Action Steps in the chapter titled *start small* in the *Greatness Habit Five* section of this book. As you plan your day, use a small Post-it note to write down the three small steps you will take first and update these three Next Action Steps throughout the day. Think of this as starting your engine. These will be the next three things you do as soon as you finish your Own Your Day morning practice.

Update these throughout the day to refocus your attention and stay in momentum.

upgrade your day

At the end of each day, the Upgrade Your Day daily practice gives you the space to debrief and celebrate your daily productivity in one little tool that will just take a few minutes. Think of it as something to look forward to at the end of each day, like dessert after a lovely dinner. The whole process will take you anywhere from 5 to 15 minutes to complete each day. Find just the right place to do it within your evening routine. For me, the trick is finding the time to do it, where it's close enough to the end of the day but not too far toward the end of the day that I'm falling asleep while I'm doing it, although that has happened a couple of times.

Purchase a *Daily Momentum 30 Day Planner* with the worksheets and prompts for Upgrade Your Day and all four pages of the Daily Momentum practice for thirty days at
www.thegetitdonesystem.com

Daily Page 4 | MAKE TOMORROW BETTER THAN TO-DAY

Daily Rewind

I first introduced you to the idea of a Daily Rewind in the chapter titled *daily rewind* within the section of this book on *Greatness Habit Three*. This simple tool will help you streamline your schedule and eliminate time wasters like a pro as you rewind and debrief your day. At the end of the day (before you get too tired), write down everything you did in your Daily Rewind. Put as much detail as possible.

Daily WINS

Taking inventory of all the WINS that happen each day is a great way to discover what makes you happy, practice gratitude, and invite more wins into your life. Remind yourself all about this powerful tool by revisiting the chapter titled *wins* in the section of this book all about *Greatness Habit One*.

After you have done your Daily Rewind, write down your Daily Wins. It is much easier to recognize wins after you have done your Daily Rewind. When jotting down your wins, consider good things that happened in all areas of your life (not just work).

12 Life Areas

1. Love

2. Self-Care

3. Spirituality

4. Growth and Learning

5. Mindset

6. Play

7. Family

8. Friendship

9. Community

10. Wealth

11. Physical Environment

12. Career and Work

Daily Debrief

Remind yourself all about how and why to use the Daily Debrief tool by reviewing the chapter titled *daily debrief* in the section of this book about *Greatness Habit Three*. Here is a quick recap.

Take a moment to recognize:

- Three things that felt satisfying today

- The top three things that you put energy into today

Daily Satisfaction Score

All we have to do to leverage the power of the Daily Satisfaction Quiz is to grade ourselves from 1–5 in each of the Six Areas of Satisfaction at the end of each day. If you would like to refresh your memory about this simple yet powerful quiz, you can revisit the chapter titled *metrics of greatness* in the section of this book about *Greatness Habit Five*.

Here is a quick recap of the Six Areas of Satisfaction:

1. Accomplishment (finishing things)

2. Space (not rushing and room to breathe)

3. Progress (moving forward toward our bigger goals and projects)

4. Focus (uninterrupted time on one thing at a time)

5. Freedom (to do whatever we want or to do things in the way we want)

6. Fun (happiness, growth, and a sense of connection)

I have created an easy way for you to take the quiz online; it even adds up your score and gives you a daily percentage.
Find the online Daily Satisfaction Quiz here:
www.dailymomentumhub.com

How to Score:

Score each of the Six Areas of Satisfaction from 1–5.

- A score of 1 would mean not at all satisfied.

- A score of 5 would indicate extremely satisfied.

- Add up and write down your total score.

- If you prefer to see things as a percentage, you can add up your score.

DAILY MOMENTUM | KEEPING SCORE

DAILY SATISFACTION QUIZ

 All we have to do to leverage the power of the Daily Satisfaction Quiz is to grade ourselves from 1-5 in each of the Six Areas of Satisfaction at the end of each day.

- A score of 1 would mean not at all satisfied.
- A score of 5 would indicate extremely satisfied.

If you prefer to see things as a percentage, you can add up your score and then divide it by .03 to get your daily percentage instead.

YOUR DAILY MOMENTUM HABIT
WWW.GETITDONEDIVA.COM

Daily Do-Over

Create new choice points in the future by writing down things you would do differently if you had a do-over for your Daily Do-Over. Each day, identify one to three different areas where you can make new choices and create new possibilities in the future. Be as specific as possible.

Remind yourself all about how to do your Daily Do-Over by rereading the chapter titled *daily do-overs* in the section of this book about *Greatness Habit Three*.

Purchase a *Daily Momentum 30 Day Planner* with all four pages of the Daily Momentum process for thirty days at www.thegetitdonesystem.com

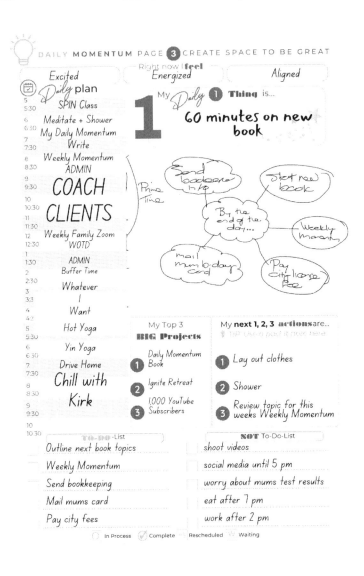

DAILY **MOMENTUM** PAGE ③ CREATE SPACE TO BE GREAT

Right now I **feel**

Excited | Energized | Aligned

Daily plan

5
5:30   SPIN Class
6   Meditate + Shower
6:30   My Daily Momentum
7
7:30   Write
8   Weekly Momentum
8:30   ADMIN
9
9:30   **COACH**
10
10:30   **CLIENTS**
11
11:30   Weekly Family Zoom
12   WOTD
12:30
1
1:30   ADMIN
2   Buffer Time
2:30
3   Whatever
3:3
4   I
4:2   Want
5   Hot Yoga
5:30
6   Yin Yoga
6:30
7   Drive Home
7:30
8   **Chill with**
8:30
9   **Kirk**
9:30
10
10:30

My Daily ① Thing is...

60 minutes on new book

My Top 3 **BIG Projects**

① Daily Momentum Book
② Ignite Retreat
③ 1,000 YouTube Subscribers

My **next 1, 2, 3 actions** are...

① Lay out clothes
② Shower
③ Review topic for this weeks Weekly Momentum

TO-DO-List

Outline next book topics
Weekly Momentum
Send bookkeeping
Mail mums card
Pay city fees

NOT To-Do-List

shoot videos
social media until 5 pm
worry about mums test results
eat after 7 pm
work after 2 pm

In Process   Complete   Rescheduled   Waiting

Start Your Daily Momentum Practice Today

So, there you have it. Own Your Day in the morning and Upgrade Your Day in the evening. You have everything you need to begin your Daily Momentum practice today.

Both the Own Your Day and the Upgrade Your Day tools are part of a planner I have designed called *Daily Momentum 30 Day Planner*. This powerful planner includes enough space for thirty days, so it works perfectly to keep you in momentum for one month.

Download a cheat sheet for your Daily Momentum practice at www.dailymomentumhub.com
Find out more about the *Daily Momentum 30 Day Planner* at www.thegetitdonesystem.com

being
extraordinary

"I'm free to be the greatest, I'm alive, I'm free to be the greatest here tonight, the greatest, the greatest, the greatest alive."

—Sia

Who do you know that is great? How do you know they are great? Is it the car they drive? The clothes they wear? The letters after their name? The position or title they hold? Is it how much money they have in the bank? Is it how many followers they have on social media?

Take a moment to think about how you measure greatness in yourself and others.

In *The Breakfast Club*, a classic '80s movie about high school, the main characters were labeled as:

- The Criminal

- The Princess

- The Brain

- The Athlete

- The Basketcase

They labeled both themselves and each other and put themselves into boxes that they couldn't see out of. This is human nature. We feel a need to label things because we think it will make life easier to organize. We really struggle when we can't easily label or put something or someone neatly into a box.

You have likely labeled me already: British, crazy, full of herself, or maybe a new friend.

Success is a label we use frequently in our lives. It gives us a sense of how we are doing. We create a pecking order in our mind and then look at where we fit into it. Then we base our actions on this illusive and intangible thing called "success."

The funny thing is, when it comes down to it, I don't know about you, but I have no idea exactly what success is! I kept finding that every time I seemed to get my hands on it, it slipped away.

Is it possible that success is NOT a thing? But then what is it? What if success is a feeling, a way of being? And what if all the cool stuff like money, recognition, or toys just naturally show up when we change the way we show up?

What if success happens when we align more with our greatness?

What if success is an inside job and all we have to do is step into our greatness to create the space to allow it in?

This is what I have come to believe. I've been fascinated by success since I was eight years old when my Grandma Ada took me to the village library to see a play. As we took our seats, I was surprised and delighted to be cast as one of the characters in the interactive production.

My love for performing began at that moment. I studied, rehearsed, and performed non-stop for two decades on small stages, in big city productions, and in front of the camera. As I spent thousands of hours in acting class, I learned to notice what brought a performance to life. As an actress, you may put on a costume; however, true talent comes forth when you are able to reveal yourself and let the audience into your soul. When a performer does this, we cannot take our eyes off them. It's extraordinary, and it happens on stage and in life when we are truly present in the moment. Since the first time I witnessed it, I have been infatuated by the rush of being present and conscious in my life!

Being in the moment is tricky to attain though. It's not easy to get into and even harder to stay in. On stage, I was hungry to feel more of it, and on my quest, I would often feel disappointment, failure, and frustration. After a performance, I would walk off stage, take off my costume, and put back on all my masks and layers of armor to protect myself in the real world.

Growing up in a country where alcohol was an accepted part of the social landscape, I began drinking at the age of eleven. So, as I struggled with my role in the real world, I turned to alcohol to find fleeting moments of freedom from the frustration and failure I was feeling. The price I paid was high. In between alcohol-based euphoria, my lows become too hard for me to handle.

At the age of 19, I attempted suicide twice. When that didn't work, I graduated to drugs and more alcohol. Then, when all else failed, I ran away to America. Los Angeles is home to many seekers of success. I sought success in film, TV, relationships, business, and friendships. What I didn't realize at the time was that I was just chasing the labels of success, recognition, and stardom, and it was never enough.

As my 40th birthday approached, I was happily married, a new mum, and a business owner. I was also spending most of my time unconscious. I would drink two liters or more of wine every evening till I blacked out and then get up the next day to do it again.

I wanted to escape from my addiction, and yet I couldn't seem to find my way out. Until one weekend, my husband and daughter were leaving to visit his family and I decided to stay behind. As I stood at the doorway to say goodbye, I kissed my husband and leaned in. I looked him in the eye. "I am going to figure this out," I told him. We both knew what I meant, and no more words were needed.

That weekend, I fought for freedom. I sat myself down and asked questions furiously. I faced my fears and created an opening for my greatness to begin to shine though. I threw off the masks, faced my truths, and never looked back.

Showing up in the world as yourself without hiding feels uncomfortable and scary, but I now realize that is what the arising of greatness within feels like.

If you look at men and women who are great, those who stand out and do remarkable things, they show us what greatness is. Greatness is not just about words; it is the power we tap into when we align our words with our actions and our truth. It is extraordinary. Greatness is to face the truth and ordinariness of who you are rather than to shy away from it. It takes courage and insight to start where you are. It takes a hunger to know thyself and to operate in the world from that place of truth. It takes tenacity to keep getting up and showing up even when you feel like you are just banging your head against a brick wall. But even in the adversity, uncomfortableness, and struggle of being great, there is still profound joy—the joy of being true to yourself that will empower you to keep going.

I believe everyone can be great. It may be at your fingertips daily or it may be buried so deep it's perhaps hard to know if it's there, but it is there. When was the last time you had a moment of truly being yourself, standing in your truth, and acting in alignment with it? A moment of intense desire, a hunger that pulled you forward? When was the last time that, instead of shying away from who you are, you magnified the greatness of it?

Was it two seconds ago, two minutes, two days, or two decades?

In acting, there are long periods of rehearsal that precede the actual performance. Hours and hours, late nights, and weeks of rehearsal. Rehearsal is where you experiment, play with choices, mess up, and figure out how to be more YOU in the role. The irony is that the performance time, even if you add up the entire run of a show, is short compared with the amount of time invested in rehearsal. I find it interesting that life and business have no rehearsal time. We are expected to get it right the first time, not make mistakes, and hit our mark without rehearsal. With so much pressure, no wonder so many people fail, run away, and feel incredible stress in their lives and businesses.

I am fascinated by the idea of helping other people fully embrace their greatness.

I created the Women's Business Momentum Center to serve this purpose. I wanted to create a space for women to learn the tools and steps they need to be great in business and in life and to practice them. Most importantly, I wanted to provide a place to fail forward in the pursuit of greatness, a space to nurture greatness and to celebrate and support it.

I have had the honor of working with hundreds of women over the last two decades at the Women's Business Momentum Center. I have watched them unlock their greatness and shine bright in the world. I have created a safe environment for them to fail and to keep getting up and showing up—to embrace, magnify, and share their uniqueness and build their lives around it. And, in doing so, to stand out as great leaders and experts in their communities, big and small.

The Momentum Squad

You can find out more about this amazing community and learn how to join at www.getitdonediva.com

It takes courage to be great. In history, great people have been ostracized, ridiculed, and resisted for their "new," big, and different ideas. Often, those same people are recognized years later for their accomplishments, dedication, breakthroughs, and courage—like Joan of Arc, Martin Luther King, Gandhi, and many of the unrecognized extraordinary men and women like you shining their light of greatness in the world today.

Great people do not walk on water; they struggle, face challenges, and encounter resistance just like everyone else. The difference is that they choose to start where they are, know what they want, make tomorrow better than today, create the space to be great, and think big, start small, and be consistent.

Greatness doesn't happen overnight, but it doesn't have to be rocket science. All it takes is Daily Momentum. You've got this. Now take it and run with it—you'll be great!